SPECTRUM®

Science

Grade 5

Spectrum®

An imprint of Carson-Dellosa Publishing LLC
Greensboro, North Carolina

Spectrum®
An imprint of Carson-Dellosa Publishing LLC
P.O. Box 35665
Greensboro, NC 27425 USA

ISBN 0-7696-5365-0

06-153127811

Table of Contents

Chapter 4 Earth and Space Science

Chapter 5 Science and Technology

Chapter 6 Science in Personal and Social Perspectives

Chapter 7 History and Nature of Science

Lesson 1.1 — Weather Trackers

barometric pressure: also called *atmospheric pressure*; the weight of air pressing down on a particular part of Earth's surface

data: facts that can be used for calculating or reasoning

proof: evidence that shows something to be true or correct

conclusions: decisions reached by using careful thought and reasoning

analyze: study or find out how different pieces of information relate to one another

Graphic organizers let you see how different pieces of information compare or relate to each other. Pie charts, flow charts, bar graphs, and line graphs are just a few of the most common types of graphic organizers.

What kinds of patterns do meteorologists look for to predict the weather?

For three weeks, the students in Mr. Klein's science class observed the weather. Each day, they recorded the highest temperature, **barometric pressure**, and wind speed. They also noted what the sky looked like and the amount of rain that fell. Mr. Klein stressed how important it was to collect good **data**.

"If you take sloppy notes," he explained, "or, even worse, just try to remember what you saw, your research won't be reliable. **Proof** is the key to science. Your records will be used to support your **conclusions**. A good scientist never says 'just trust me, I know.' He or she backs up every claim with evidence."

The class had been divided into several groups. Each group tracked one aspect of the weather. Today, they were copying all their research into one big chart. Then, the class would **analyze** the information and draw conclusions.

The first group went to the board and filled in each day's temperature on the chart. Another group added descriptions of the sky—cloudy, partly cloudy, or clear. One by one, the groups completed the weather chart.

The final group was in charge of barometric pressure. Each day, they had read a barometer placed inside the classroom. Its needle pointed to a number between 28 and 31.

"A barometer measures atmospheric pressure," Mr. Klein had explained. "The air around you is filled with molecules made of nitrogen, oxygen, and other elements. If you step outside and look up into the sky, every inch of that space contains molecules. All those molecules added together create a lot of weight pressing down on your body.

"Molecules aren't spread evenly through the atmosphere, though. Sometimes, the air above you weighs more than it does at other times. The amount of pressure weighing down on Earth's surface—and us—changes. The barometer takes a measurement of that pressure. Our hypothesis will be that barometric pressure gets lower when it's going to rain."

Day 1		Day 2		Day 3		Day 4		Day 5		Day 6		Day 7	
74°	30.5	78°	30.8	75°	30.2	70°	29.4	70°	28.9	68°	28.5	65°	28.3
5 mph	0"	4 mph	0"	6 mph	0"	8 mph	0"	11 mph	0"	15 mph	.5"	22 mph	1"
Clear		Clear		Clear		P. Cloudy		P. Cloudy		Cloudy		Cloudy	
Day 8		**Day 9**		**Day 10**		**Day 11**		**Day 12**		**Day 13**		**Day 14**	
66°	28.6	72°	30.1	74°	30.4	80°	30.0	76°	29.3	72°	28.7	74°	29.5
10 mph	.25"	8 mph	0"	8 mph	0"	4 mph	0"	9 mph	0"	8 mph	.25"	15 mph	0"
Cloudy		P. Cloudy		Clear		Clear		Cloudy		Cloudy		P. Cloudy	
Day 15		**Day 16**		**Day 17**		**Day 18**		**Day 19**		**Day 20**		**Day 21**	
77°	31.0	81°	30.4	72°	29.5	72°	29.3	69°	28.9	67°	29.5	70°	29.8
18 mph	0"	6 mph	0"	10 mph	0"	12 mph	0"	14 mph	.5"	12 mph	0"	17 mph	0"
Clear		Clear		P. Cloudy		Cloudy		Cloudy		Cloudy		P. Cloudy	

Use the chart on page 6 to answer the following questions.

1. Which day was coldest? _day 7_

2. Which day was warmest? _day 16_

3. Which day was the windiest? _day 7_

4. Which days were the least windy? _day 2 and 11_

5. What was the total amount of rainfall during this three-week period? _6.5 in_

Write **true** or **false** next to each statement below.

6. _false_ The windiest days always occurred when it was raining.

7. _False_ The barometric pressure seldom changed.

8. _true_ The lowest temperatures usually came on cloudy days.

9. _true_ The barometric pressure was at its highest on clear days.

Write your answers on the lines below.

10. Can this chart be used to predict the weather for the next month? Why or why not?

    No because weather cant form
    diffrent weather.

11. Did the information gathered by the students prove or disprove their hypothesis? Explain your answer.

    The kids hypothesis proved when the
    heat went down it did rain.

What's Next?

For one week, watch the weather report on the evening news each day. What information does the meteorologist include in his or her report? Do you see similar patterns in how the weather changes in your area compared to what the students in this selection observed?

characteristics: the qualities that make something different from others; traits

offspring: the young of an organism

pollinated: fertilized; transferred grains of pollen from the male to the female parts of plants

variables: parts of an experiment that can change and cause a change in the results

traits: the qualities that make something different from others; characteristics

crossbreeding: breeding two different types of plants with one another

genes: the parts of a plant or animal that determine what traits will be passed on to the offspring

Mendel had hoped to become a high school teacher. He took the exam several times and failed it, so he continued his work as a monk and did experiments in his spare time.

Mendel experimented with about 30,000 pea plants in order to discover the laws of heredity, or how traits are passed along.

How did the study of pea plants lead to the discovery of how traits are passed from one generation to the next?

Gregor Mendel was an Austrian monk who was very interested in plants. He spent much of his time in the monastery's garden. Mendel was curious about the **characteristics** of different plants and their **offspring**, so in 1857, he decided to breed peas. He chose to study seven characteristics of the pea plants, such as the length of the stem and the color of the ripe seeds. First, he made sure that the plants he was studying were purebred. This meant that they always had offspring with the same characteristics. If a plant had wrinkled seeds, its offspring would have wrinkled seeds, too.

He also used a greenhouse because he didn't want his plants to be **pollinated** by insects. This would have introduced too many **variables**. For the purposes of the experiment, Mendel had to control the pollination himself.

The first results didn't surprise Mendel. It made sense that a young plant would have the same **traits**, or characteristics, as its parents. Next, Mendel tried **crossbreeding** pea plants that had different traits. For example, he bred a plant that had a long stem with one that had a short stem. What kind of plants do you think he got? Ones that had a medium-length stem? Mendel was surprised to see that all the offspring had long stems. It seemed as though the shortness characteristic had disappeared. When he tried breeding these new plants with one another, he found that some of their offspring were tall and some were short. What was going on?

Mendel kept experimenting and discovered that pairs of **genes** determine each characteristic—one gene from each parent. Some traits are stronger than others. He called these *dominant traits* and called the weaker ones *recessive traits*. Mendel used a capital letter as a symbol for a dominant trait, and a lowercase letter as a symbol for a recessive trait. Two dominant genes (TT) or one recessive and one dominant gene (Tt) would result in offspring having the dominant trait. Only when the offspring received two recessive genes (tt) would it have the recessive trait.

Mendel was right, but it took almost 40 years for others to believe him. He tried to share the results of his work, but no one took him seriously. He was only an amateur scientist, not a professional. Today, Mendel is known as the "father of genetics."

	Maternal	
	T	**t**
T	TT	Tt
t	Tt	tt

(Paternal)

Circle the letter of the best answer to each question below.

1. Which of the following is a human trait?

   a. eye color

   b. height ⟵ (circled)

   c. hair texture

   d. All of the above

2. A hypothesis is a statement that is assumed to be true so that it can be tested. Which of the following might have been one of Mendel's hypotheses?

   a. Two purebred plants will have offspring that have the same traits as they do. (circled)

   b. Plants with long stems produce more peas.

   c. Pea plants with short stems cannot have offspring.

   d. Why are some traits stronger than others?

Write your answers on the lines below.

3. In a certain type of plant, the gene for red flowers is dominant and the gene for yellow flowers is recessive. If a purebred plant with red flowers was crossed with a purebred plant with yellow flowers, what color flowers would the offspring have?

   Orange

4. If **F** is the dominant red flower gene and **f** is the recessive yellow flower gene, what color is each of the flowers listed below?

   FF: _red_   ff: _yellow_   Ff: _red_

5. Why do you think Mendel needed to be in charge of the pollination of his pea plants?

   Because he wanted to keep an eye on them.

6. Why didn't other scientists take Mendel's work seriously?

   He was not a professional at his work

7. What would have happened if other scientists had tried performing Mendel's experiments themselves?

   They would have done it very.

Break It Down

process: series of
events that lead to a
certain result

erosion: the
movement of rock and
soil by natural means,
such as wind and rain

mechanical
weathering: the
breaking apart of rock
into smaller pieces by
physical forces

chemical
weathering: the
breaking apart of rock
into smaller pieces by
chemical forces

The Mississippi River
carries an average of
230 million tons of
eroded material into
the Gulf of Mexico
each year.

The roots of plants
and trees help hold
soil in place. They
also offer the soil
some protection from
wind. As human
beings have used
more land for
agriculture and
building, they have
cut down trees. This
causes the land to
erode more quickly
than it might have
otherwise.

What processes cause changes in Earth's surface to take place?

The surface of Earth is constantly changing. This might surprise you. After all, hills, valleys, and rivers don't appear to change much at all from day to day or even year to year. That's because most changes to Earth's surface happen slowly. They are part of a **process** called **erosion**. Erosion is the natural movement of rocks and soil over time. Agents of erosion—the forces that move the material—are water, wind, and ice.

Wind can't move an enormous boulder, though. Water can't wash away an entire mountain. Before the forces of nature can move anything, weathering must take place. Weathering is a process in which rock is broken down into smaller pieces. Weathering and erosion are both natural processes, or series of events that lead to the changing of the landscape.

When physical forces act on rock, **mechanical weathering** is taking place. Water is a common cause of mechanical weathering. Water can cause rocks to break apart, through rain or ocean waves. Water also seeps into tiny holes in rocks. When it freezes, it expands and puts pressure on the rock, which causes it to crack and break apart.

Glaciers—huge masses of ice, snow, and rock—move very slowly. As they do, they grind and scrape away at layers of rock. Even trees and animals can be sources of weathering. An animal that uses its claws to burrow underground can break rocks into smaller pieces. The roots of trees can do the same thing over time.

Chemical weathering causes a change to the minerals that are found in rocks. It breaks down the bonds that hold rocks together. For example, rain absorbs carbon dioxide as it falls through the air. It forms an acid that eats away at certain types of rocks.

Once material has been weathered, it is carried away, often by water. The water can be in the form of rain that beats against a cliff or ocean waves that pound on a coastline. It can be a stream whose movement pulls pebbles and silt from its banks and carries them along. Wind can also pick up soil, tiny bits of rock, and sand and transport them from one place to another.

The changes brought about by weathering and erosion are usually slow. A big storm, like a hurricane can speed them along. Otherwise, you must be patient and observant to see the landscape change.

Circle the letter of the best answer to each question below.

1. Which of the following is an agent of erosion?

   a. thunder

   b. ocean waves *(circled)*

   c. glaciers

   d. Both b and c

2. What is the result of the processes of weathering and erosion?

   a. changes to the landscape *(circled)*

   b. the formation of larger mountains

   c. more flooding during times of heavy rains

   d. overflowing rivers and streams *(circled)*

Write your answers on the lines below.

3. Explain how weathering and erosion are different from one another.

   Weathering breaks down erosion and picks
   _it up."_

4. How is the freezing and thawing of water a part of the weathering process?

   Because ice freezing and crackes into smaller
   peices of ice

5. What is one effect that human beings have had on erosion?

   Him or her Sictnes.

6. How would a storm like a hurricane or a tornado speed up the process of erosion?

   The wind blowedpick up more alot faster.

7. How is a glacier a source of both weathering and erosion?

   Glacier freezes by water and moves by erison

What's Next?

Arizona's Grand Canyon, which is more than 5,000 feet deep, was formed by erosion. See if you can find out what forces created this spectacular beauty. How long did it take?

Taking Heat

thermal energy: the amount of heat energy stored inside a substance

scales: ways of taking measurements using a series or sequence of equal units

properties: special qualities of a substance or substances

absolute zero: 0 K, or the temperature at which no heat energy is present; it exists only in theory and has never been reached; it is equal to -459.67°F

The coldest temperature ever found in nature is 1 K, or about -457°F. It was measured in the Boomerang Nebula, about 5,000 light-years from Earth.

To change a temperature from Celsius to Fahrenheit, multiply the Celsius temperature by 1.8 (°C x 1.8) and then add 32.

To change a temperature from Fahrenheit to Celsius, subtract 32 from the Fahrenheit temperature (°F - 32) and then multiply the result by 0.56.

What does a thermometer really measure?

A rock on the ground doesn't seem like a very energetic thing. If you could see its atoms and molecules, though, you'd know differently. All those tiny particles are bouncing around, giving the rock plenty of energy. Pick up a rock that's been warmed by the sun, and you'll feel some of this energy.

Heat causes atoms and molecules to move more quickly. The heat you feel coming from the rock is actually energy causing the atoms and molecules in your hand to pick up speed. Heat is energy moving from one place to another.

Everything contains atoms and molecules in motion, so everything has energy. How hot or cold something is—the amount of energy it has— depends on how quickly or slowly its particles move. This means that when you measure temperature, you are really measuring moving molecules. You're measuring how much energy something has.

Thermometers are the scientific tools used to measure temperature. They can use mercury, electricity, or electromagnetic waves to see how much **thermal energy** something has. Several different **scales** have been developed for thermometers.

You are probably most familiar with temperatures given in the Fahrenheit scale. The German physicist Daniel Fahrenheit invented this method in 1724. No one knows for sure what he based his scale on. One guess is that he set 0°F as the lowest temperature he recorded during winter, and 100°F as the temperature of his body. On the Fahrenheit scale, water freezes at 32°F and boils at 212°F. Today, the United States is the only country that still regularly uses Fahrenheit temperatures.

The rest of the world—and most scientists—use the Celsius scale, named after Swedish astronomer Anders Celsius. The Celsius scale is based on **properties** of water. On Earth, water is the only substance that exists naturally in three states of matter—solid, liquid, and gas. The Celsius scale is based on this characteristic of water. Water freezes at 0°C and boils at 100°C.

Another temperature scale that some scientists use is the Kelvin scale. Each Kelvin is equal to one degree Celsius, but the Kelvin scale starts at a much lower temperature—**absolute zero**. At absolute zero, atoms and molecules stop moving completely because they have no thermal energy. This is only an idea, though. Atoms and molecules never really stop moving.

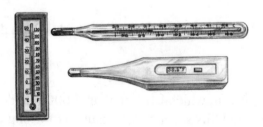

Circle the letter of the best answer to each question below.

1. All matter has _energy_ because everything contains atoms and molecules in motion

   a. energy

   b. frequency

   c. kelvins

   d. properties

2. Heat is

   a. not found in cold things.

   b. another word for atoms and molecules.

   c. a way to measure temperature.

   d. energy on the move.

3. What does a thermometer measure?

   a. water

   b. thermal energy

   c. temperature

   d. Both b and c

Write your answers on the lines below.

4. Why are 0° and 100° important in the Celsius scale?

   0° freezes and 100° boils.

5. How is the Kelvin scale different from the Celsius scale? How are they similar?

   Because a Kelvin scale is equal to one Celsius. Celsius is based on water.

6. What is absolute zero?

   Atoms that stop molecules from moving.

7. If it's 58°F outside, what is the temperature in degrees Celsius? Use a calculator if you need help.

   14.56°C

   58 −
   32
   26

engineers: people who design and build things

practical: useful; not just experimental

mechanisms: the parts that allow a machine to work

rudder: a flat, movable piece of wood or metal used for steering a ship or airplane

propeller: blades attached to a central point that spins; used to propel boats or airplanes

To this day, almost all airplanes are still steered using the design invented by the Wright Brothers.

For several years, most people doubted that the Wright Brothers' flight really happened. Only a few witnesses were at the beach that day. A few months later, the brothers tried to fly again in Ohio. This time, with plenty of reporters watching, the Wright Brothers' machine could barely get off the ground.

"Genius is one percent inspiration and ninety-nine percent perspiration."— Thomas Edison, inventor

What does it take to become a famous inventor?

In the late 1800s, Wilbur and Orville Wright owned a bicycle shop in Dayton, Ohio. The men even designed their own brand of bicycle. With the money they made, the brothers began working on something they loved even more than bicycles—flying machines.

The Wright Brothers had been closely following the work of other inventors and **engineers**. They had read about Otto Lilienthal's successful—and dangerous—glider flights in Germany. They were excited by Samuel Langley's flying, steam-powered models. They had heard reports about Octave Chanute's glider experiments over the sand dunes of Lake Michigan. All of this had happened in a single year—1896. A real race was on to invent the perfect flying machine. The Wright Brothers wanted to join in.

The brothers soon realized that getting human beings into the air wasn't the problem. Machines could already do that. They could even fly around for a while. The problem was that they were impossible to control. This point was made tragically clear when Lilienthal was killed in a glider crash that same year. The Wright Brothers knew that the key to inventing a **practical** flying machine was finding a good way to steer it.

For the next five years, the men designed and tested hundreds of different wing shapes and steering **mechanisms**. They tested their gliders in the steady winds blowing across the flat beaches at Kitty Hawk, North Carolina.

In 1901, the brothers thought they had a glider that would work perfectly. They tested it dozens of times, only to discover that it still wasn't right. Disappointed, they headed back to Ohio to keep trying.

Finally, they had a breakthrough. By adding a **rudder** to the glider's tail, it could be steered using both the wings and the tail. When they tested this new glider design in 1902, it steered safely over the sand dunes.

The next year they focused on designing an engine for their glider. By the time they headed back to Kitty Hawk, their flying machine had an engine and a **propeller**.

For weeks they tried unsuccessfully to get their plane into the air. The propeller kept breaking, and they had engine troubles. Finally, on December 17, 1903, the Wright Brothers made history. Their machine flew straight into the wind for hundreds of feet. Human beings have been flying ever since.

Circle the letter of the best answer to each question below.

1. The Wright Brothers' mechanical skills were _____

    a. learned in the army.

    b. **first used for constructing bicycles.**

    c. not good enough to build a working airplane.

    d. used to build steam engines.

2. What key problem did the Wright Brothers concentrate on solving?

    a. **controlling the flying machine when it was in the air**

    b. getting the flying machine off the ground with a person inside

    c. finding a good fuel for the flying machine's engine

    d. finding the best place to test their flying machines

Write your answers on the lines below.

3. Why was Kitty Hawk a good place to test flying machines?

    They had flat beaches.

4. Do you think the Wright Brothers invented every mechanism in their flying machine? Why or why not?

    No because it did not stay in the air as long as they wanted.

5. Were the Wright Brothers good scientists? Give at least two reasons that support your answer.

    Yes because they studyed flight and worked on bikes.

Unifying Concepts and Processes

How do you think the invention of automobiles was similar to the invention of airplanes? How was it different?

    Because both have engines.

Safety First

precautions: safety measures

contaminated: made impure or unusable

dispose: to throw out or get rid of

Professional scientists often need special protection when they are working. For example, astronauts wear spacesuits that have more than 10 layers of material. The suits keep astronauts safe from the harsh conditions of space.

Marie Curie was a scientist best known for her work with radiation. At the time, no one yet knew about the dangers of radioactive materials, so Curie did not take proper safety precautions. She was even known to carry test tubes of these harmful materials in her pockets. Marie Curie died of leukemia at the age of 66 from her exposure to radiation.

How can you keep yourself and your environment safe when you are performing scientific investigations?

Performing experiments and doing scientific research can be exciting and interesting. There can be risks, though, so it's important that you take **precautions**—whether you're at home or at school.

- Some science projects are safe to work on alone. For others, you should have an adult's supervision. Before you start any experiment or project, check with an adult.

- Reading directions carefully is a must. Read the entire instructions thoroughly before you begin, and make sure you understand them as well as any possible dangers.

- Protect yourself. If you'll be using chemicals, you should wear safety glasses and gloves. The safety glasses can also protect your eyes if there's a chance something might explode or shatter. An apron can protect your clothing and body. If you have long hair, be sure to keep it tied back. Also, remember not to wear sandals or open-toed shoes in the lab, especially when you're working with chemicals, materials that become hot, or heavy objects. If you're wearing loose clothing or dangling jewelry, make sure that it is secured before you begin working.

- Don't bring food or anything to drink into a lab. There's always the risk that it could become **contaminated**. You could end up consuming something that is harmful.

- Don't experiment with chemicals if you're not sure what reaction might take place. Many chemicals become dangerous when combined. For example, bleach and ammonia form a poisonous gas.

- If you are collecting specimens in nature, such as plants or leaves, be sure to clean your hands and nails thoroughly afterward. Some species are poisonous or can cause allergic reactions.

- Water conducts electricity. If you are working with electrical equipment, make sure your hands and your workspace are dry.

- Be careful of how you **dispose** of materials. Chemicals, plant or animal materials, and samples of bacteria should not be placed in a household or school trash can. Check with a teacher or parent to find out how to safely get rid of these materials.

- If you use a hot plate or a Bunsen burner, double-check that it is turned off when you have finished with it.

1. Erika is getting ready to test how several different chemical solutions react with one another. List all the safety problems you see in the picture.

Loose clothing, food, open shoes, no safetey glasses, dangaling jewlery.

Write **true** or **false** next to each statement below.

2. ____true____ Working with water and electricity at the same time is dangerous.

3. ____false____ If an experiment is intended for kids, no adult supervision is needed.

4. ____false____ As long as you are in a lab, it is safe to mix any kinds of chemicals together.

5. ____true____ Not all scientific materials can be thrown directly in a trashcan.

Write your answers on the lines below.

6. What are three types of protective coverings that can be used when working in a lab?

Saftey glasses   _Saftey clothing_   _Safety apron_

7. Why is it important to read through the instructions before beginning an experiment?

Because if you do it wrong something will go wrong.

8. Ms. Khoury is going to demonstrate to the class how to make ice cream using liquid nitrogen, a substance with a temperature of less than -300°F. Liquid nitrogen can freeze skin tissue and cause great damage. What precautions does Ms. Khoury need to take?

Warm gloves full sheet of warmth.

habitable: able to be lived in or support life

atmospheric signature: the combination of chemicals that make up a planet's atmosphere

exoplanet: also called *extrasolar planet*; a planet beyond our solar system that orbits a star other than the sun

"Science does not know its debt to imagination."—Ralph Waldo Emerson, author and philosopher

Sara Seager is an astronomer and professor of planetary science at Massachusetts Institute of Technology (MIT). She is best known for her work on extrasolar planets. The models she makes give scientists an idea of what planets outside our solar system might be like. Her research led to the first discovery of an exoplanet atmosphere in 2001. Seager has been awarded several prizes and honors for her work in this field.

What are exoplanets? Why does astronomer Sara Seager search for them?

Why did you choose to search for planets outside our solar system?

Sara Seager: I always loved astronomy, and the search for planets seems like a tremendously exciting thing to do. The prospect of finding a **habitable** planet is already within reach of current technology and is something I look forward to every day.

Why is discovering an atmosphere on another planet such an important find?

SS: The **atmospheric signature** gives us clues to the gases in the atmosphere and whether or not life is present. For example, oxygen is not natural to our atmosphere but is created by plants. If we could detect oxygen or ozone gas in a distant exoplanet atmosphere, we would have a sign that life might be present. Similarly, the best sign we have of the existence of liquid water oceans is a great deal of water vapor in a planet's atmosphere. This is important because all life as we know it requires liquid water.

Do you think life exists somewhere outside our solar system?

SS: Absolutely. There are 100 billion stars in our own galaxy and possibly as many as 100 billion galaxies. Some stars must have Earth-like planets and some of those planets are very likely to have life.

What traits do you have that make you a good scientist?

SS: The creative ability to ask good questions which become research projects, the ability to focus and get things done, and technical skills for my chosen field of research.

What is the most important scientific tool you use? Why?

SS: Without a doubt, my computer is the most important scientific tool I use. I make computer models of **exoplanet** atmospheres and interiors, using basic physics and chemistry. I can run my exoplanet models again and again, like running a different experiment many times. I use the results to interpret observations of new exoplanets and for predictions of what is to come.

Why did you decide to become a scientist?

SS: I love trying to answer questions, and I had a talent for logical thinking.

Do you have any advice for students who are thinking about a career in science?

SS: Study all of the basic maths and sciences, as you never know which subject will be useful in the future. Try to meet a scientist who can show you around his or her lab. It is important to know that the daily life of a scientist is very different from just learning science in school.

Use the words in the box to complete the sentences below.

| ~~atmosphere~~ | ~~exoplanets~~ | ~~technology~~ | ~~habitable~~ |

1. One day, Seager hopes to find a ___habitable___ planet that can support life.

2. Gases in a planet's ___atmosphere___ can be a sign to whether or not life exists on the planet.

3. ___technology___ allows Seager to create models of planets beyond our solar system.

4. ___Exoplanets___ orbit stars other than the sun.

Write your answers on the lines below.

5. Why do you think creativity is an important quality of a good scientist?

   Because it will give good idea's.

6. Why do scientists look for water vapor, ozone, or oxygen in a planet's atmosphere?

   If there's life on that planet there should be oxegen.

7. Name two pieces of advice that Seager has for students who are interested in becoming scientists.

   Study Math and science.

8. Why does Seager think that life exists outside our solar system?

   Cause theres millions of

9. Why is a computer such an important tool in Seager's work?

   Computer's have intele on alot of things

Unifying Concepts and Processes

The models that Seager creates allow her to predict what the atmosphere on other planets might be like. Explain why prediction can be an important element of scientific inquiry and investigation.

   The tool can see long long long ways away.

NAME _Malachi_

Circle the letter of the best answer to each question below.

1. Why did Mendel grow his pea plants in a greenhouse?

   a. because they received better light

   b. because there wasn't enough room in the garden

   c. because the greenhouse protected the plants from bad weather

   d. because he didn't want insects to pollinate them with pollen from other types of peas

2. Which of the following is not a process?

   a. weathering

   b. water

   c. erosion

   d. growth

3. In order to create a flying machine, the Wright Brothers

   a. conducted experiments.

   b. made observations.

   c. collected data.

   d. All of the above

4. What will most likely happen if the barometric pressure drops below 29?

   a. It will start raining.

   b. It will be a sunny day.

   c. It will be windy.

   d. A high-pressure system will enter the area.

Write your answers on the lines below.

5. Why is it important for a scientist to take careful notes and record his or her data?

   So they can study and learn more about that subject

6. Why did it take so long for Mendel's work on genetics to be recognized by the scientific community?

   Because he took a long time studying plants.

7. Explain how weathering and erosion are related.

Weathering breaks up erison into smaller peices.

8. The Celsius scale is based on properties of _water_.

9. Why is absolute zero only an idea and not something that exists in nature?

Because it breaks down moleculese.

10. Give one reason why the Wright Brothers became the first people to invent a practical flying machine.

Because they knew if they did not try they would not make it happen.

11. Name three safety precautions you should follow when working in a science lab.

Dangaling neckleses, long clothes, and open shoes.

12. What is one possible conclusion that a scientist can draw after finding oxygen or water vapor in a planet's atmosphere?

life on that planet.

Use the words in the box to complete the sentences below.

conclusions	practical	genes	analyze	contaminated	energy

13. Food and drink can become _Contaminated_ if they are brought into a lab.

14. Heat is _energy_ moving from one place to another.

15. Scientists use their observations and the evidence they collect to reach _Conclusions_.

16. _Genes_ determine which characteristics a person, plant, or animal will have.

17. Inventions are created all the time, but only the _practical_ ones become part of everyday life.

18. Scientists _analyze_ data to see if their hypotheses are correct.

Lesson 2.1   The Anatomy of an Atom

elements: substances that contain only one kind of atom and cannot be broken down further using ordinary chemical methods

matter: substances that have mass and take up space in the visible universe

nucleus: the central part of an atom; it contains nearly all of an atom's mass in the form of protons and neutrons

subatomic: relating to things inside an atom or smaller than an atom

charge: an amount of electricity

ions: atoms with positive or negative charges

Hydrogen atoms are the simplest kinds of atoms. Each hydrogen atom has just one proton and one electron. Unlike other atoms, hydrogen doesn't have any neutrons.

An atom's mass is made up almost entirely from its neutrons and protons. Electrons are so tiny that they have barely any mass at all.

What goes on inside an atom?

Elements were discovered by breaking down **matter** into simpler forms. Elements are substances that have only one kind of atom, such as an iron atom or oxygen atom. For example, rock, which is matter, can contain iron, oxygen, silicon, and carbon atoms, which are elements.

As small as atoms are, they aren't the smallest pieces of matter. Every atom is made of even tinier particles called *protons*, *neutrons*, and *electrons*.

The structure of each kind of atom is basically the same. At the center is a **nucleus**. Neutrons and protons are huddled together in the nucleus. The electrons form a sort of atmosphere around the nucleus.

Elements are different from one another because each kind of atom has different amounts of these **subatomic** particles. For example, a helium atom has two protons, two neutrons, and two electrons. An argon atom, though, has 18 protons, 22 neutrons, and 18 electrons.

A normal atom is balanced. In other words, it has equal numbers of protons and electrons. Many atoms, however, become unbalanced easily. Electricity is the result of atoms that aren't balanced.

Each proton in an atom's nucleus has a positive **charge**. Each electron whirling around the outside has a negative charge. Neutrons don't have any charges. As long as the atom has equal amounts of electrons and protons, their charges cancel each other, and the atom itself has no charge. The number of neutrons is sometimes, but not always, equal to the number of protons.

Many atoms have trouble hanging on to their electrons, though. They gain and lose electrons pretty easily. Atoms with unequal amounts of electrons and protons are called **ions**. An ion with too many electrons has a negative charge, and an ion with too few electrons has a positive charge.

Negative ions share their extra electrons. They give them away to the atoms that need them. It's no coincidence that the words *electron* and *electricity* are similar—the flow of electrons is electricity.

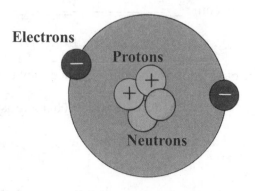

Circle the letter of the best answer to each question below.

1. Which of the following would not be found in an atom?

   a. a proton

   b. an ion

   c. an electron

   d. an electrical charge

2. Each carbon atom has six protons. What does this tell you?

   a. Each carbon atom has six electrons.

   b. Each carbon atom has six neutrons.

   c. Each carbon atom has three electrons and three neutrons.

   d. Both a and b

3. Each element

   a. has only one kind of atom.

   b. has only one kind of molecule.

   c. is made of rock.

   d. All of the above

Write your answers on the lines below.

4. What is the nucleus of an atom?

   _____

5. Explain why electrical charges flow from one atom to another.

   _____

   _____

6. Why are hydrogen atoms different from the atoms of all other elements?

   _____

7. Name three elements that were mentioned in this selection.

   _____   _____   _____

Opposites Attract

neutral: having no electrical charge

friction: the force that keeps two things from moving smoothly against each other

repel: to force away or drive apart

exposed: left without protection or cover

The atoms of certain materials gain or lose electrons more easily than others. For example, hair and wool lose electrons easily. Materials like rubber, nylon, and plastic gain electrons easily.

When you drag your feet across carpet, the friction causes electrons to move from the carpet, into your socks, and then into your feet. The extra electrons give your body a negative charge. When you touch something made of a good conductor, like metal, the charges burst out at once, giving you a small electrical shock.

Why does a dryer cause static cling?

As Ms. McNulty's students entered the classroom, they found her eating a bowl of cereal. Puffy cereal was scattered across the table.

Ms. McNulty brought a balloon out from underneath the table. Several students giggled, wondering what she was up to.

The teacher waved the balloon a couple of inches above the spilled cereal. Then, she grinned at the class and began rubbing the balloon against her hair. After half a minute, Ms. McNulty pulled the balloon away. Everyone started laughing, as some of her hair tried to come along with it.

Ms. McNulty held the balloon over the cereal again. This time, cereal jumped and bounced against the balloon. A few pieces stuck for a second before falling back to the table. Ms. McNulty finally spoke to her class.

"Yesterday, we learned that atoms have electrons, protons, and neutrons," she began. "Does anyone remember what I said about electrical charges?"

"Each electron has a negative charge," one student answered. "Each proton has a positive charge. Atoms usually have equal amounts of both, so the charges cancel each other, making the atoms **neutral**."

"Atoms also gain and lose electrons easily," Ms. McNulty continued. "Rubbing the balloon against my head created **friction**, which caused electrons to move from my hair's atoms into the balloon's atoms. All those extra electrons caused the balloon's atoms to have negative charges.

"Remember that opposites attract. Opposite charges pull toward each other, but like charges **repel**. The extra electrons in the balloon repelled the electrons in the cereal's atoms. Once the cereal's electrons were moved out of the way, the protons in its nucleus were **exposed**. The positive charges in the cereal's protons were attracted to the negative charges in the balloon's electrons. This attraction was strong enough to cause the cereal to jump toward and stick to the balloon.

"When the cereal touched the balloon, though, it picked up some of the balloon's extra electrons. The piece of cereal and balloon both had negative charges, so they repelled each other. The cereal shot back down to the table.

"Now, " Ms. McNulty said, "let's clean up this mess."

Circle the letter of the best answer to the question below.

1. An atom with the same number of electrons and protons

    a. will also have the same number of neutrons.

    b. will not have an electrical charge.

    c. will have a neutral charge.

    d. Both b and c

Choose a word or words from the box to complete each sentence below.

electrons	electricity	negative	attract
friction	positive	protons	repel

2. Electrons have a _____ charge, and protons have a _____ charge.

3. Rubbing two materials together creates _____, which causes electrons to move.

4. _____ is electrons moving from one atom to another.

5. An atom will have a negative charge if it has more _____ than

    _____.

6. Positive charges _____ negative charges, but two negative charges will

    _____ each other.

Write your answer on the lines below.

7. Using information from the selection, explain why wool socks that have just come out of a clothes dryer will stick to a pair of nylon running pants.

    _____

    _____

Unifying Concepts and Processes

Sometimes, when a person pulls a sweater over his or her head, friction causes electrons to move from the hair into the sweater, causing the hairs to stand on end and look like they're floating in air. Why do you think the hairs won't lie flat together? Hint: After losing some of their electrons, what does each hair have in common?

radiating: sending out rays or waves

electromagnetic field: areas in space that contain electromagnetic radiation

radiation: the process of giving off energy in the form of waves or particles

conductor: a material or substance through which an electrical current can pass

The electromagnetic spectrum is the entire range of electromagnetic waves. It includes everything from giant radio waves to tiny gamma rays, including visible light.

Radio waves can be created with electricity. Each time an electrical current is turned off or on, it emits a wave. When the current is turned off and on repeatedly, a series of waves is created. A radio transmitter creates these waves and then adds coded messages to them. A radio receiver captures the waves and then reads the message they contain.

What is the electromagnetic spectrum?

In 1820, Danish physicist Hans Christian Oersted made an interesting observation. When he placed a compass near a wire carrying an electrical current, the compass's needle moved toward the wire. As soon as he turned the current off, the needle pointed north again. Oersted saw that electricity and magnetism were related, but he wasn't sure how.

Ten years later, British physicist Michael Faraday proved that Oersted's discovery worked in the opposite direction, too. Faraday put a magnet near a wire attached to a meter. The meter showed that an electrical current moved through the wire, even though it wasn't connected to any electrical source. The magnet was causing electrons to flow inside the wire.

Faraday also showed that electricity flowing in one wire would cause a current to move in another wire placed next to it. Some kind of invisible energy was **radiating** from the magnets and the electrified wires. This energy could create more electricity and magnetism. Faraday had discovered **electromagnetic fields**. Like light glowing from a light bulb or heat flowing from a hot sidewalk, electromagnetic fields surround magnets and electrical currents.

Another British physicist, James Clerk Maxwell, suggested that this electromagnetic energy was shaped like waves. Maxwell soon realized that light—which he knew also moved like a wave—was a kind of electromagnetic energy as well.

The atom's structure was unknown in Maxwell's time, so he didn't know exactly what was happening. When electrons flow through a wire, their movement sends out waves of energy, or **radiation**. These waves create an electromagnetic field, which acts like a magnet and can create an electrical current. For example, when a magnet is placed near a wire made of a good **conductor**, like copper, energy from the magnet's field causes electrons to move in the wire. It creates an electrical current.

Electromagnetism has proven to be one of science's most important discoveries. Light, heat, microwaves, radio waves, and x-rays are all waves of electromagnetic energy. Electromagnetism may even be the link connecting everything in the universe.

Circle the letter of the best answer to each question below.

1. Electricity and magnetism
   a. were invented by James Clerk Maxwell.
   b. are related to one another.
   c. both move through wires.
   d. work together to create electrons.

2. Electromagnetism is a form of
   a. energy.
   b. light.
   c. atom.
   d. All of the above

3. What is light?
   a. energy in the form of a wave
   b. magnetism
   c. electricity
   d. electrons moving through space

4. Electromagnetic fields surround
   a. magnets.
   b. electrical currents.
   c. waves.
   d. Both a and b

Write your answer on the line below.

5. Name two forms of electromagnetic energy.

   _____

What's Next?

When you think of radiation, you probably think of nuclear energy or atomic bombs. Anything that gives off waves of energy, though, is producing radiation. Find a chart showing the electromagnetic spectrum. Everything listed in the spectrum is a type of radiation, although some kinds are harmless and others are dangerous. Find out which waves in the spectrum you should avoid and which kinds are safe.

Full of Energy

kinetic energy: the energy of an object in motion

potential energy: energy waiting to be released

compressed: pressed together

converted: changed from one form into another

All molecules contain stored energy called *chemical potential energy*. When chemical bonds are changed, this energy can be released. Gasoline is one example of chemical potential energy. When gasoline is burned, it releases energy that can power a car, a lawnmower, or a plane.

Amusement parks are great places to learn about energy. For example, roller coaster cars must be pulled up the first hill. As they move higher and higher, they gather potential energy. When the cars reach the top of the hill, gravity pulls on them. The potential energy is converted to kinetic energy, and the coaster cars go rushing down the hill at high speeds.

What is energy?

Energy is everywhere—it's in your body, your home, your car. Energy is the ability to do work and to set things in motion. The two main types of energy are kinetic and potential. **Kinetic energy** is the energy an object has when it is moving. A person dancing, a baseball flying through the air, and a waterfall are all examples of kinetic energy. **Potential energy** is energy waiting to be released. An object like a **compressed** spring has potential energy because of its position. Think of an orange balanced at the edge of a table. The orange has potential energy. As soon as you push it and it begins to fall, the potential energy is **converted** into kinetic energy.

Tasha and Connor were ready to try their experiment. They had all the materials they needed. Now, all they had to do was set things up. Tasha propped a piece of plywood against the edge of the kitchen table to make a ramp. Connor put a small empty coffee can on the floor at the bottom of the ramp. Beside the coffee can, he placed a yardstick.

"Don't forget," Tasha reminded Connor. "We need to weigh the balls before we start."

Connor took three steel balls of different sizes out of a plastic bag. He balanced the first one on the scale. "This one weighs three ounces," he said. Tasha made a note of that and handed him the other two balls.

"This one weighs six ounces, and the largest one weighs nine ounces," he reported.

"Okay," said Tasha, "let's see what they can do." She positioned the smallest ball at the top of the ramp. "Right now, ball 1 has potential energy," she said. She let go. "Now it has kinetic energy," she said, as she watched it roll swiftly down the ramp and push the coffee can aside.

"It moved the can five centimeters," said Connor.

Tasha and Connor repeated the experiment two more times, using the other steel balls. Ball 2, which weighed six ounces, pushed the coffee can nine centimeters, and ball 3 pushed it 17 centimeters.

"Our hypothesis was confirmed!" cheered Tasha. "The larger balls, the ones with greater weight, had more potential energy. They pushed the coffee can farther."

Circle the letter of the best answer to each question below.

1. According to Tasha and Connor's experiment, which of the following is true?

   a. The greater an object's mass or weight, the less potential energy it has.

   b. The greater an object's mass or weight, the greater its potential energy.

   c. An object with a small mass has no potential energy.

   d. Both b and c

2. Which of the following is not an example of kinetic energy?

   a. a car speeding down the street

   b. wind turning a windmill

   c. a boy sinking a basketball in a hoop

   d. a pebble sitting on the ground

Write your answers on the lines below.

3. When Tasha positioned a steel ball at the top of the ramp, it had gravitational potential energy. The pull of gravity on the ball changed the object's potential energy to kinetic energy. Give another example of something that has gravitational potential energy.

   _____

   _____

4. Why do you think food is a source of chemical potential energy?

   _____

   _____

5. At summer camp, Emma is learning how to use a bow and arrow. When she pulls back on the bow,

   what kind of energy does it have? _____

   Once she releases the bow and the arrow flies toward its target, what kind of energy does it have?

   _____

6. In terms of energy, what happens when you push down on a spring?

   _____

An Elegant Arrangement

The periodic table also divides the elements into families. Here are a few of them:

Noble gases:
Also called *inert gases*—*inert* means "slow or unable to react." They're in column eight, which tells you that they already have eight electrons filling up their outer shells. It's rare for them to be part of chemical reactions or to combine with other atoms in molecules.

Alkali metals:
Alkali metals are in column one. They have only one electron in their outer shells. This means they tend to be very reactive, because they easily combine with atoms from other columns.

Transition metals:
These metals are where the periodic table gets complicated. They can share electrons from their two outermost shells. They can also hold up to 32 electrons in some of their shells.

Why is the periodic table such an important tool?

In the 1800s, Dmitri Mendeleyev was searching for a better way to list the elements in a logical order. He looked at their physical and chemical properties and soon realized that they could be arranged neatly into a chart. The periodic table of the elements—used today by chemists everywhere—is based on Mendeleyev's work.

The elements are placed into the table in order of their atomic numbers. An element's atomic number tells how many protons are inside each of its atoms. The periodic table also divides the elements into rows and columns, based on the number of shells the element has.

The electrons moving around an atom's nucleus don't share the same orbit. They are divided into orbitals, or shells. Think of them like layers in an onion. Each shell can hold only a certain number of electrons. The inner shell holds just two, but the next shell can hold as many as eight electrons. The third shell can hold 18 electrons and the fourth can hold 32.

Helium, for example, has two electrons. It needs just one shell. Oxygen has eight electrons. Its inner shell holds two, and its outer shell holds the other six. The outer shell isn't full, though. Remember, it can hold up to eight electrons.

Each row of the periodic table tells how many shells an atom needs to hold its electrons. Aluminum, with atomic number 13, is in the third row. It needs three shells of orbiting electrons—two fill the inner shell, eight fill the next shell, and three electrons orbit in the outer shell.

Each column of the periodic table tells how many electrons are in an atom's outer shell. Atoms in the first column have just one electron in their outer shells. Atoms in the fifth column have five electrons in their outer shells.

Atoms try to fill their shells with electrons. This is why molecules form and chemical reactions happen—atoms combine with other atoms so they can share electrons and fill their outer shells.

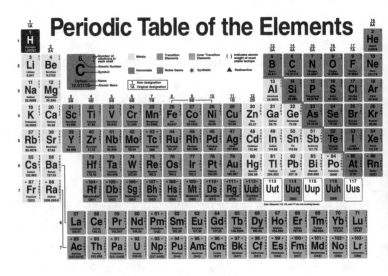

Circle the letter of the best answer to each question below.

1. The periodic table does not tell you

   a. each element's atomic number.

   b. which family an element belongs to.

   c. the temperature at which an element will melt.

   d. how many electrons are in each kind of atom.

2. The number of electrons in an atom's outer shell determines which _____ it's in.

   a. column

   b. family

   c. row

   d. table

Write your answers on the lines below.

3. How many electrons can each shell of an atom hold?

   Shell closest to the nucleus: _____

   Second shell away from the nucleus: _____

   Third shell away from the nucleus: _____

4. What is the first element that needs a third shell?

   _____

5. Sodium is listed in column one because it has a single electron in its outer shell. Chlorine, in column seven, has seven electrons in its outer shell. Sodium and chlorine atoms often combine to form the common molecule NaCL, also known as *table salt*. They share their electrons so that the outer shell is full with eight electrons. Another common molecule is H_2O. Explain why oxygen atoms easily combine with two hydrogen atoms.

   _____

   _____

Mercury: The Liquid Metal

fluid: flow or move like a liquid or gas

bonded: held or linked together chemically

mined: taken from the ground

toxic: poisonous

Mercury's chemical symbol is Hg, which stand for *hydrargyrum*, a Greek word meaning "watery silver."

Mercury's atomic number is 80, which means that it has 80 protons in its nucleus.

During the 1800s, mercury was commonly used to make felt for hats. Hat makers often breathed in toxic levels of mercury fumes during their lives. One effect of mercury poisoning is mental illness. This is where the term "mad as a hatter" comes from. It inspired the Mad Hatter character from Lewis Carroll's *Alice's Adventures in Wonderland*.

When is a metal not solid?

Human beings have discovered or created 117 different elements. Three-quarters of them are metals. You probably think of metal as something shiny and solid that's used to build cars and skyscrapers. Most metals do share these physical characteristics, along with being good conductors of electricity and melting at high temperatures. Mercury is different from other metals because it is a liquid at normal room temperature.

Mercury is sometimes called *quicksilver* because it looks a bit like melted silver. If you pour mercury onto a table, it flows across the surface just like spilled water. How can mercury be both a metal and a liquid?

Most metallic elements are solids. The molecules and atoms inside a solid fit together like the pieces of a puzzle. These particles are still moving, but it's a vibrating motion—they don't float freely like the particles in liquids and gases do. When you touch a solid, your fingers don't go through it because the atoms and molecules are locked together.

The particles in liquids are much less densely packed together. When you touch a liquid, the atoms and molecules are **fluid**, so they move out of the way. Your hand plunges right into the substance. Gases are even less dense. The particles drift around with very little connection to each other. You can walk right through a gas and not even notice.

Mercury is a liquid because its atoms are **bonded** more loosely than other kinds of metals. Of course, like any element, mercury becomes a solid if the temperature drops low enough. Mercury is one of only five elements that are liquids at average Earth temperatures. Most elements are solids at these temperatures, and about 20 are gases.

Mercury is still a metal, though, because it's shiny and it conducts electricity. It also reacts chemically with oxygen, which is something else metals do.

Mercury is one of the rarest elements in Earth's crust. Human beings have already **mined** most of it. Elements don't disappear, though. Mercury is still in Earth's environment. It's released into the air when coal and trash are burned. Mercury from thermometers, batteries, and light bulbs gets into the ground when these things are thrown away. Mercury is **toxic**, so we have to be careful how it's used—and even more careful about where it ends up.

Circle the letter of the best answer to each question below.

1. Mercury's chemical symbol is

   a. Me

   b. Mr

   c. Hg

   d. Hm

2. Which of the following statements is not true?

   a. At room temperature, mercury is a liquid.

   b. The atoms and molecules in a gas move freely.

   c. The molecules in a solid do not move.

   d. Mercury is a good conductor.

3. On Earth, most of the elements are

   a. metals.

   b. solids.

   c. good conductors.

   d. All of the above

Write your answers on the lines below.

4. List three characteristics of metals.

   _____   _____   _____

5. Mercury's atomic number is 80, so how many protons does a mercury atom have?

   _____

6. Give two reasons why mercury isn't used as often today as it once was.

   _____

   _____

7. Explain why you can't stick your hand through something solid, like a wall.

   _____

   _____

sound: energy that travels in waves away from a vibrating object

mediums: materials, like solids, liquids, or gases, through which sound waves travel

amplitude: the distance between the crest and trough of a wave; determines loudness

decibels: units of measurement for sound

frequency: the number of waves that pass a point in a certain amount of time

Sound travels through the air at a speed of about 340 meters (1,120 feet) per second. That might seem fast, but light travels more than a million times faster.

There is no atmosphere in space, so there is no sound. Without molecules of matter to vibrate, sound can't happen.

An echo is a repeated sound. It is caused by sound waves that reflect off a surface. Echoes are often heard in canyons, valleys, or caves, when sound waves bounce off the walls.

What is sound, and how does it travel?

The world is filled with sounds—the chirping of birds, the hum of a dishwasher, the wail of a siren, the slam of a car door. Pure silence is hard to come by. Even in the middle of the night, you can usually hear the ticking of a clock or the buzz of faraway traffic.

Sound is a form of energy that is made by vibrations. It travels in waves away from the object that created it. Sound energy causes the molecules that make up all matter to vibrate. As they vibrate, they produce a wave that carries, or transmits, the energy.

Sound travels through some **mediums** better than others. In a solid, like a piece of metal, the molecules are packed tightly together, so sound is transmitted easily. The molecules are spaced farther apart in a liquid, like water, and even farther apart in a gas, like the air we breathe. That's why sound travels more than three times faster through water than it does through air.

The crest is the highest point on a wave, and the trough is the lowest point. The distance between two crests is called the *wavelength*. The distance between a crest and a trough is called **amplitude**. The amplitude is the loudness of a wave. This can be measured in **decibels**. A sound that can barely be heard—like the hum of a computer—measures around zero decibels. A sound that it is so loud that it hurts your ears—a jackhammer or a stereo turned all the way up—measures 120 decibels or more.

If you could see sound waves, you'd notice right away that they don't all look alike. One difference you might notice is in **frequency,** or the number of waves that pass a point in a certain amount of time. High-pitched sounds have a higher frequency than low-pitched sounds. The sound waves made by a girl's voice are spaced more closely together than those made by a man with a deep voice.

Have you ever thought of what the difference is between sound we call *noise* and sound we call *music*? Noise is random sounds. They aren't organized in patterns, and they don't have rhythm. Music is sound that has pitch, rhythm, and organization. Music and noise both create sound waves—it's mostly the way that people interpret those waves that is different.

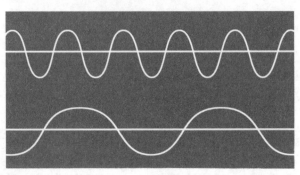

Circle the letter of the best answer to the question below.

1. What is sound?

   a. the vibration of matter

   b. electricity

   c. energy

   d. Both a and c

Write your answers on the lines below.

2. Explain why sound travels faster through water than through air.

   _____

   _____

3. As it travels farther from its source, a sound wave spreads out. How do you think this affects its amplitude?

   _____

4. Not everyone has the same definitions of what noise is and what music is. Think of an example of a noise that has a pattern. Could it be considered music? If so, in what way?

   _____

   _____

Use the words in the box to label each part of the diagram below.

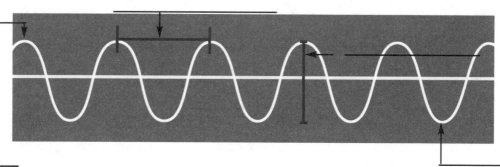

| crest | amplitude | wavelength | trough |

What's Next?

Wrap a piece of tissue paper around the end of a cardboard paper towel tube and secure it with a rubber band. Sing or hum into the tube, and see if you can feel the tissue paper vibrating. Try changing the pitch of your voice. Do you notice a change in the vibrations?

NAME _____

Review

1. Label the three types of particles found in the lithium atom below.

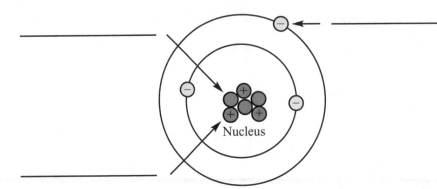

Circle the letter of the best answer to each question below.

2. An ion is

   a. the same thing as an electron.

   b. an atom with an electrical charge.

   c. electrons in motion.

   d. an atom without any neutrons.

3. What is electromagnetism?

   a. the spectrum of waves

   b. radiation

   c. a form of energy

   d. All of the above

4. The periodic table shows how _____ relate to each other.

   a. elements

   b. molecules

   c. minerals

   d. All of the above

5. A hydrogen atom is different from other atoms because

   a. it is magnetic.

   b. it has an electrical charge.

   c. it doesn't have any neutrons.

   d. it doesn't combine with other atoms to form molecules.

Write **true** or **false** next to each statement below.

6. _____ Friction causes protons to move from one atom to another.

7. _____ Atoms usually have equal amounts of protons and electrons.

8. _____ Pushing a pen off a desk converts potential energy to kinetic energy.

9. _____ When an atom has more electrons than protons, it has a negative charge.

10. _____ All atoms have eight electrons in their outer shell.

11. _____ Sounds travel better through gases than they do through solids.

Write your answers on the lines below.

12. What is electricity?

_____

13. What does it mean to say that opposites attract when you are talking about atoms?

_____

14. What happens when a magnet is placed near a copper wire?

_____

15. Explain the difference between potential and kinetic energy.

_____

_____

16. What does an element's atomic number tell you?

_____

17. What makes mercury different from most metals?

_____

18. Most elements are _____, and at the temperatures found on Earth, they are also

_____.

19. What is sound?

_____

Lesson 3.1 | Life in the Grasslands

biome: a community of organisms living in a particular climate that depend on one another

savanna: a tropical grassland

drought: a period of little or no rain

parasites: organisms that live in or on other organisms

scavengers: animals that eat the remains of prey they did not kill

If an ostrich thinks its young are in danger, it will act injured. Once the predator has been lured away, the ostrich can usually outrun it. Ostriches can run at speeds of 40 miles per hour—faster than most predators, except the cheetah.

How do the animals of the African savannas depend on one another?

What do rain forests, deserts, and oceans have in common? They are all examples of biomes found around the world. A **biome** is a large community of plants and animals living in a certain climate that interact with one another. A **savanna** is a tropical biome that contains grasses, shrubs, and scattered trees. Nearly half of Africa is savanna—about five million square miles. The African savannas have a long wet season every year. It is followed by a shorter dry season, which is often a time of **drought**.

There is huge diversity of life in the savanna. Serengeti National Park, which is mostly grassland, is home to 35 species of mammals and more than 500 species of birds. Each type of animal has a role to play in the complex relationships found in life on the grasslands.

Termites are some of the smallest members of the savanna biome. They are part of the diet of many creatures, including the aardwolf, a shy relative of the hyena. With its long, sticky tongue, an aardwolf may consume hundreds of thousands of termites in a day. Other animals, like birds and snakes, find shelter in the tall mounds termites build. Some even move into a mound after the termites have abandoned it.

Rhinoceroses have a relationship with several different types of savanna birds. They allow birds, like egrets and oxpeckers, to perch on their backs and feed on the **parasites** living there. The birds get a free meal, and the rhinos rid themselves of the tiny, pesky organisms.

Large predators, like lions and cheetahs, provide food for many grassland animals. The big cats are skillful hunters. Other animals, like vultures, marabou storks, and hyenas, are **scavengers** that eat the carrion, or leftover meat from a predator's kill. A bird called the *ground hornbill* not only eats carrion but also consumes the insects that come to feed on it.

Herd animals, such as ostriches, zebra, and wildebeest, are often prey for grassland hunters. They work together to protect themselves from the hungry predators. Ostriches have good eyesight—their eyes are nearly the size of tennis balls—and many of the hoofed animals have a good sense of smell. Together, they can sometimes spot a predator before it reaches the herd.

Life in the African savanna is like a giant machine. Each of the pieces of the machine—the plants and animals—must do their part to help the machine function and maintain nature's delicate balance.

Circle the letter of the best answer to the question below.

1. One key element of all biomes is that

    a. they contain few living things.

    b. the plants and animals depend on one another.

    c. they all contain grasses and a large body of water.

    d. Both b and c

Write your answers on the lines below.

2. What role do termites play in the African savanna?

    _____

    _____

3. Explain the relationship rhinoceroses have with birds such as egrets.

    _____

    _____

4. What is a savanna? Describe the physical characteristics, and name several types of animals found there.

    _____

    _____

    _____

5. Why is every plant and animal in a biome important?

    _____

What's Next?

Many of the animals that live in the African savanna are endangered. What threats do they face? What role do human beings play? Are they the reason these animals are endangered, or are they trying to help save them? Do some research online or at the library. See what you can find out about the state of animals in the African savanna today and their future.

Bringing Back the Wolves

predator: an animal that hunts and eats other animals

coexist: to live in peace with one another

eradicate: to completely get rid of something

reintroduce: to release animals from captivity back into the wild

Back in their natural habitat, wolves are an important part of their ecosystem. Every plant and animal in an ecosystem plays a role. Wolves are at the top of the food chain. When they disappeared, populations of other animals, like elk, grew larger. There wasn't always enough plant material to keep them alive, and after a rough winter, many starved to death. Coyotes also became more widespread because they didn't have to compete with wolves. This had an effect on the food chain, too, because the smaller animals that coyotes prey on were harder hit.

Why did wolves nearly disappear from the U.S.? Why are they making a comeback?

People have always had strong feelings about wolves. Some think they are beautiful wild animals that should be protected. Others find them to be a fierce and threatening **predator**. Thousands of wolves used to roam the United States. When settlers started moving west, they had to **coexist** with these wild creatures. Wolves sometimes attacked and killed livestock, so ranchers quickly grew to hate them. They trapped and killed wolves in large numbers. Even the U.S. government agreed with the plan to **eradicate**, or get rid of, all the remaining wolves. By the 1970s, only about 500 wolves remained in the United States, outside of Alaska.

In 1973, the Endangered Species Act was passed. It's no surprise that wolves were on the list of animals that were in danger of becoming extinct. Over time, the views of many people, as well as the federal government, began to change. In 1994, the Yellowstone Wolf Project was born. The goal of the project was to **reintroduce** wolves to Yellowstone, a national park located in Wyoming, Idaho, and Montana.

Ranchers were worried about the safety of their livestock, just as their ancestors had been. In spite of their objections, wolves were reintroduced. A team from the U.S. Fish and Wildlife Service worked with trappers in Canada to find wolves that would adapt well to life in Yellowstone. They had to be used to living in a cold, mountainous environment. They also had to know how to hunt elk—a major part of their Yellowstone diet.

A total of 66 wolves were trapped in Canada and brought to the U.S. They were kept in pens for a while so that they could form family groups called *packs*. Wolves are social creatures that are very loyal to their packs. The trappers had been able to capture only one or two wolves out of a pack, so they needed the wolves to form new packs before their release.

The plan has been a success. The number of wolves has increased to about 3,500—better than anyone had hoped. There have been some attacks on livestock because the wolves have spread to areas outside of the park. Ranchers are given money to make up for any animals they lose to wolves. It's not an ideal situation, but once again human beings and wolves are able to share the land and live side by side.

Circle the letter of the best answer to each question below.

1. The wolves that were reintroduced to Yellowstone

   a. were used to living in warm climates.

   b. showed no interest in harming livestock.

   c. knew how to hunt elk.

   d. Both a and c

2. Why has the Yellowstone Wolf Project been considered a success?

   a. because the wolves live only within the boundaries of Yellowstone

   b. because ranchers and farmers no longer hate wolves

   c. because the wolves are no longer killing any livestock

   d. because the wolves that were reintroduced are surviving and breeding

Write your answers on the lines below.

3. What was the main reason that people wanted to eradicate wolves?

   _____

4. What effect did the loss of wolves have on the food chain?

   _____

   _____

5. What does it mean to say that wolves are social creatures?

   _____

6. Do you think it was the right decision to reintroduce wolves in the West? Explain.

   _____

   _____

What's Next?

Wolves aren't the only animals that have been reintroduced to their natural habitat. Search online and see what other animals you can find that have been reintroduced. How did the reintroduction affect the animal's ecosystem? Did people have as strong feelings about it as they did about the reintroduction of wolves to Yellowstone?

The Green Desert

harsh: severe and difficult

adapted: changed to fit into a specific situation or environment

water table: where water is found below ground; wells are dug to reach the water table

dormant: growth or other biological activities are suspended

ecosystem: community of living things that interact with each other

Giant saguaro cacti of the American West are very successful desert inhabitants. Their huge, thick bodies hold incredible amounts of water. Bats feed on nectar from the saguaro's flowers. Woodpeckers carve out nests in their bodies. Once the woodpeckers move to new nests, tiny owls take over the old ones. Because saguaros can live for more than 200 years, a single saguaro cactus might provide a home for thousands of animals.

What kind of plants can grow in a desert?

The scorching sun beats down, and the temperature soars to 110°F. A steamy breeze blows across the dry ground. Deserts are **harsh** places, but about one-fifth of Earth's surface is covered with them. An area is considered desert if it receives less than ten inches of rainfall per year.

Most people picture sand when they think of a desert, but only a few of Earth's deserts are completely covered in sand. Most of them have a thin layer of soil mixed with stone and gravel. Deserts are also known for their hot temperatures, but they can get very cold at night. Because the air is so dry, there is no moisture to hold the sun's heat overnight. Once the sun sets, temperatures can fall to 30 or 40°F.

It's hard to imagine plants growing in a place with so little water, but desert plants have characteristics that allow them to survive. Some of them have **adapted** by growing long roots. For example, the mesquite tree has roots that snake deep below ground in search of a water source. Their roots can grow 50 feet or more trying to tap into the **water table**.

Plants lose moisture through their green surfaces. For this reason, plants with lots of leaves can't usually survive in the desert because each leaf adds to a plant's total surface area. Cacti do well in a dry environment because they are thick and solid. They have less surface area that loses water, and their thick bodies can store a lot of moisture.

Some desert plants survive by staying **dormant** most of the time. Ocotillo usually looks like a dried-up, dead plant. As soon as it rains, though, the gray, spiky stems change dramatically. Within just a few days, tiny green leaves pop up among the spines, and little red flowers bloom at the ends of each stalk. After a few weeks, the leaves get yellow and fall to the ground, and the ocotillo goes dormant again until the next rain.

Plants play an important role in the desert **ecosystem**. Animals rely on them for food and shelter, like they do in most places on Earth. In the desert, though, plants provide water, too. For example, the desert agave, or century plant, is filled with moisture. When the desert is at its driest, many animals eat agave stems for the liquid inside.

Circle the letter of the best answer to the question below.

1. All deserts are

    a. hot.

    b. dry.

    c. sandy.

    d. All of the above

Write your answers on the lines below.

2. What is one characteristic that desert plants developed so they could survive in a dry environment? How does this characteristic help the plant?

    _____

    _____

3. Explain why there aren't very many trees in deserts.

    _____

    _____

4. What role does the saguaro cactus play in its ecosystem?

    _____

5. In the forest, many animals eat the leaves from trees. In the desert, though, most plants are covered with thorns and spikes. Why do you think this trait evolved in desert plants?

    _____

    _____

Unifying Concepts and Processes

What is another example of a plant becoming dormant? Explain why this happens.

_____

_____

A Good Relationship

anthers: the male reproductive part of a flower; produces pollen

stigma: the female reproductive part of a flower

mutualism: a relationship between organisms that has benefits for both

pollinators: animals or insects that transfer pollen from one flower to another

coevolved: changed together over time in a way that benefits both species

nectar: a sweet substance that plants produce; used by bees to make honey

Bats are nocturnal creatures, meaning they are active after dark. The flowers that bats pollinate are open at night. They tend to have large, sturdy blooms, since bats are larger than insect pollinators. They are also usually light in color and have a strong scent that helps the bats locate them.

Not all plants are pollinated by animals or insects. The wind pollinates corn, wheat, nuts, and rice.

Why do insects and flowering plants need each other?

On a sunny afternoon, you're picking some flowers from the garden. You hear a loud buzzing sound and realize that one of the flowers you just picked has a bee inside it. What was the bee doing there? It was gathering pollen, a powdery material produced by the male reproductive parts of a flower called the **anthers**.

During its visit, the bee performed a very important service for the flower. This wasn't the purpose of the bee's visit—it was only there to collect food. Honeybees have fuzzy bodies, though, and pollen sticks to the tiny hairs. When the bee flies to another flower, some of the pollen falls off and sticks to the flower's female reproductive part, the **stigma**. Now, the flower is able to produce seeds that can grow into new plants.

This kind of relationship is called **mutualism**—both the bee and the flower benefit from it. The bee is fed and pollinates a flower in the process. The flower gives up some of its pollen to the bee, but without the bee, the flower wouldn't be able to reproduce.

Bees are one of the most common and important **pollinators**. For many flowering plants, only one kind of pollinator can perform the job. Without bees, human beings' food supply would be seriously affected. Hundreds of types of fruits and vegetables would become rare and might even disappear.

Other pollinators in the natural world are moths, butterflies, wasps, and some types of flies and beetles. Even birds and bats can be pollinators. The hummingbird has an interesting relationship with a flowering plant called the *fuschia*. Scientists believe that the hummingbird and the fuschia **coevolved**, or evolved together, adapting to one another.

The hummingbird has a long, skinny beak that is perfect for sucking the **nectar** from flowers. The tiny bird doesn't have a good sense of smell, but it is attracted to the color red. The fuschia flower is long and tube-like. It doesn't have an odor, but it comes in different shades of red. There isn't really any place to land on fuschias, but this doesn't matter to hummingbirds. Their wings beat very quickly and allow them to hover in the air while they eat. Fuschias depend on hummingbirds in order to reproduce. Hummingbirds get plenty of sweet nectar from fuschia blossoms. Like many other pollinator/flower pairs in nature, they're a perfect match for each other.

Use the words in the box to complete the sentences below.

stigma	adapt	depend	pollen

1. Honeybees collect _____ on their bodies when they feed from a flower.

2. It is the job of pollinators to transfer tiny grains of pollen to a flower's _____.

3. Flowering plants _____ on insects and animals to help them reproduce themselves.

4. Some plants and insects _____ to one another over time.

Write your answers on the lines below.

5. Why is a hummingbird better suited to pollinating a fuschia flower than a bee or a bat would be?

    _____

    _____

6. Some gardeners use a cotton swab or small brush to transfer pollen from one flower in their garden

    to another. In this case, human beings are acting as _____.

7. Why do plants need to be pollinated?

    _____

Read the paragraph below, and answer the questions that follow.

   The yucca plant, which grows in the Southwest, can be pollinated only by the yucca moth. The moth lays its egg in the yucca's flower. In the process, it transfers pollen to the stigma. When the moth caterpillars hatch, they feed on some of the yucca's seeds.

8. Explain how this relationship is an example of mutualism.

    _____

    _____

9. Who is the pollinator in this example? _____

10. Do you think that yucca plants and yucca moths coevolved? Explain your answer.

    _____

    _____

Bouncing Back

echolocation: the use of sound and echoes to locate objects

emit: give off; produce

hertz: a measurement of the frequency of sound waves

echolocators: animals that use echolocation

Two types of birds, oilbirds and swiftlets, nest in caves and use echolocation to help them move in their dark environments. Shrews, a type of mammal similar to moles, use echolocation to hunt and to explore their underground habitat.

The closer an echolocator gets to an object, the more pulses it emits in short bursts. When a killer whale is close to its prey, it can send out as many as 500 pulses in a second.

Dolphins can use echolocation on targets that are both nearby and far away at the same time.

How can sound be used to locate objects in the dark?

Bats may not seem to have much in common with whales and dolphins, but they do share an important ability—**echolocation**. Echolocation is the use of sound to hunt or to move around in areas of low light.

You've already learned that sounds are vibrations that travel through matter. Animals that use echolocation **emit** very high-pitched sounds. These sound waves bounce off objects in the animal's environment and send back echoes. The animal uses the echoes to locate prey. A bat, for example, can tell where an insect is, how large it is, and in what direction it is moving, even in complete darkness. A whale using echolocation to hunt may even be able to tell the difference between types of fish.

A sound's frequency, or number of vibrations per second, is measured in **hertz**. Human beings can hear sounds between about 20 and 20,000 hertz. The sounds that dolphins and whales use in echolocation vary from about 250 hertz to 220,000 hertz. Bats emit sounds between 20,000 and 120,000 hertz. Doesn't it seem like listening to sounds at such high frequencies would damage an animal's ears? As a form of protection, a muscle in the ear keeps the damaging pulses from being transmitted into the inner ear.

It's probably hard to imagine that echoes could provide enough information for a bat to capture a tiny mosquito in the pitch-black night. **Echolocators** are very good, though, at interpreting the information they receive. The farther away an object is, the longer echoes take to come back. The echoes sound different, too, depending on the size of the object and its texture.

An echolocator doesn't actually think about the information it receives in the form of echoes. Its brain automatically does the job of processing this information with incredible speed. Think about the way your vision works. When you see something, a message is sent to your brain, and your brain decodes the images and makes sense of them. It takes so little time that it seems to happen instantly. Echolocation takes place in a similar way.

Circle the letter of the best answer to the question below.

1. Which of the following statements is true?

   a. Hertz are a measure of a sound's loudness.

   b. The echolocation sounds that bats use are too high a frequency for human beings to hear.

   c. The sound of human speech measures greater than 20,000 hertz.

   d. Both b and c

Write your answers on the lines below.

2. What are two characteristics of an object that would cause it to produce a different echo than something else?

   _____

3. In your own words, explain how echolocation works.

   _____

   _____

   _____

4. How have the bodies of echolocators adapted to the high-pitched sounds the animals emit?

   _____

5. Why do birds use echolocation?

   _____

6. There is a mosquito 10 feet away from a bat and a moth 16 feet away. When the bat emits a series of

   pulses, the echoes from the _____ will take longer to come back.

Unifying Concepts and Processes

Why do you think some animals have the ability to use echolocation while others do not? What characteristics might an animal that doesn't use echolocation have?

_____

_____

Feeling Nervous?

spinal cord: the long bundle of nerves inside the spinal column; part of the central nervous system

impulses: electrical signals

neurons: nerve cells

neurotransmitters: chemicals that help transmit nerve impulses

involuntary: done automatically, without choice or control

When you learn things, your brain creates pathways between neurons. For example, if you're trying to memorize a song on the piano, practicing will help. The more you practice, the sooner a pathway will be created. After a while, you'll be able to just sit down and play the song without even trying to remember it.

The human brain weighs only about three pounds. It has many folds and grooves, which give it plenty of space for storing information.

What role does the nervous system play in the human body?

You may not realize it, but your nervous system is hard at work all the time. One of its jobs is to keep your body safe from harm. When you touch a hot pan, you quickly pull your hand away before you even realize what has happened. That's just a small part of what the nervous system does, though. It's in charge of all your body's actions and senses. Without it, you wouldn't be alive.

There are two main parts to the nervous system. The central nervous system is made up of the brain and the **spinal cord**. The brain is the control center for your body. It uses the spinal cord to send out messages to the rest of the body. The peripheral nervous system is the huge network of nerves that runs from the spinal cord throughout your body. It carries **impulses** to and from the central nervous system.

Neurons are the tiny cells that make up the tissues of the nervous system. There are billions of neurons in the human body. All sorts of things can stimulate neurons—an odor in the air, a flash of light, a math problem, taking a deep breath. When a neuron is stimulated, it reacts by sending an electrical impulse. This impulse causes chemicals called **neurotransmitters** to be released. They help the pulse travel to the next neuron, and so on.

Think of it as a chain reaction, like pushing a single domino and watching as a whole row of dominos tumble. The reaction continues until the message gets where it needs to go. It might reach a muscle and cause you to move your arm to flick away a bug by your face. It might reach your brain and be recorded as the smell of cookies baking. The nervous system helps you receive information from your environment and communicate it around your body.

The autonomic nervous system is part of the peripheral nervous system. It is in charge of all the processes in your body that happen without your thinking about them or controlling them. These are called **involuntary** activities. For example, digestion takes place every time you eat something. You don't decide to digest something, it just happens. Your nervous system works with all your other systems and organs to help your body function.

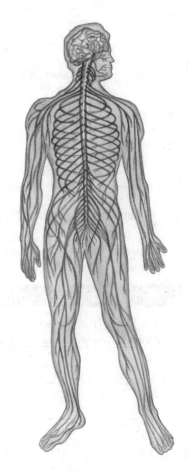

Circle the letter of the best answer to the question below.

1. The autonomic nervous system controls

   a. your ability to kick a ball.

   b. the beating of the heart.

   c. the muscles in your hand when you hold a toothbrush.

   d. the muscles that allow you to smile.

Write **true** or **false** next to each statement below.

2. _____ Neurotransmitters are the cells of the nervous system.

3. _____ Your body's nervous system is always working, even when you are asleep.

4. _____ The peripheral nervous system is made up of the spinal cord and the brain.

5. _____ The nervous system is a system of communication.

Write your answers on the lines below.

6. Name three things not mentioned in the selection that could stimulate neurons.

   _____

   _____

7. Explain what happens when you do something, like a riding a bike or reciting a poem, over and over again.

   _____

   _____

8. What is the difference between a voluntary and involuntary action? Give one example of each.

   _____

   _____

   _____

9. Explain how the nervous system uses both electrical and chemical processes to function.

   _____

   _____

Seeing Double

fraternal twins: two non-identical babies born to one mother at the same time; the result of two eggs being fertilized by two sperm cells

siblings: brothers or sisters; people who share the same parents

identical twins: two identical babies born to one mother at the same time; the result of one egg being fertilized and then dividing into two embryos

embryos: human beings in the very early stages of development

heredity: the genes and traits that are passed along from parent to child

Conjoined twins are twins whose bodies are joined at birth. If the twins do not share a vital organ, like a heart, they are usually separated by surgery.

Every summer, the Twins Day festival takes place in Twinsburg, Ohio. Twins from all over the world, and people who study them, come to this three-day gathering.

What makes two people look exactly alike?

What would it be like to be a twin? Many people have wondered this at some point in their lifetimes. Would a twin be just like you? Would he or she look the same and have the same interests and feelings? It's possible—it would depend to some degree on what type of twin it was.

Twins occur when a mother gives birth to two babies from one pregnancy. **Fraternal twins** are the most common. They may be the same gender, or there may be one boy and one girl. These twins are not any more similar to one another than any other two **siblings** are. Fraternal twins occur when two of the mother's eggs are fertilized by two different sperm cells. Like all full siblings, they share about half their genes. Male-female fraternal twins are the most common. They make up about 40% of all twins born.

Identical twins occur when a single egg is fertilized and then divides into two **embryos**. Both babies share the same set of genes. This results in siblings of the same gender who look a lot alike and often have similar personalities and interests. Identical twins are about four times less common than fraternal twins.

Studies have shown that identical twins are most alike when they are very young. As they grow older, they can develop more differences. This is because they are influenced by their environment. Even if the twins grow up in the same home with the same set of parents, they have different life experiences. People are shaped by their environments and experiences as well as by their genes.

Scientists are often very interested in studying twins who grew up apart from one another. For example, the twins may have been placed in different adoptive homes at birth. This gives scientists the perfect chance to study the effects of **heredity** versus the environment—often called *nature versus nurture*.

Scientists are curious to see how similar twins are when they grow up in different places with different parents. Findings show that genes really do shape many parts of a person's life. Time after time, identical twins who didn't even know each other existed have amazing similarities in their lives. They may have the same haircut, the same type of career, enjoy the same hobbies, and even have married similar people. These studies certainly make a strong case for the power of genes.

Write your answers on the lines below.

1. What is one way in which identical and fraternal twins are similar and one way in which they are different?

    _____

    _____

2. What is heredity?

    _____

3. Why do more differences develop between identical twins as they age?

    _____

4. Explain why identical twins are identical and fraternal twins are not.

    _____

    _____

Write **true** or **false** next to each statement below.

5. _____ Fraternal twins are always the same gender.

6. _____ Conjoined twins are born joined to one another.

7. _____ Identical twins share only about half their genes.

8. _____ Identical twins are more common than fraternal twins.

9. _____ Fraternal twins are not any more alike than any other pair of siblings.

10. _____ Genes are the only influence on a person's appearance and personality.

Unifying Concepts and Processes

Explain why scientists do studies of separated identical twins. Are there other ways they could study nature versus nurture? Why are identical twins ideal for this type of study?

_____

_____

_____

Review

Circle the letter of the best answer to each question below.

1. Which of the following is not a biome?

   a. a desert

   b. grasslands

   c. a pond

   d. the Arctic tundra

2. What was the goal of the Yellowstone Wolf Project?

   a. to eradicate wolves from Yellowstone National Park

   b. to move all the wolves from Yellowstone to Canada

   c. to use wolves to control the population of livestock in the West

   d. to reintroduce wolves to their natural habitat in the West

3. What is mutualism?

   a. a relationship between organisms that has benefits for both

   b. a relationship between organisms that benefits human beings

   c. the relationship between predator and prey

   d. the relationship between two animals that compete for food

4. What two parts of the body make up the central nervous system?

   a. the brain and the heart

   b. the brain and spinal cord

   c. nerves and the spinal cord

   d. nerves and blood vessels

5. Fraternal twins develop from

   a. the same fertilized egg.

   b. two different fertilized eggs.

   c. unfertilized eggs.

   d. eggs from two different people.

Write your answers on the lines below.

6. Explain what the relationship is between predators and scavengers in the African savanna.

_____

7. How is a savanna, or any other biome, like a machine?

_____

8. Why did some people object to wolves being reintroduced to Yellowstone?

_____

9. Why do some desert plants need extremely long root systems?

_____

10. What characteristic do cacti have that allow them to survive in deserts?

_____

11. Explain how bees pollinate flowering plants.

_____

_____

12. Explain how some animals use echolocation to hunt.

_____

_____

13. What is the role of neurons in the human body?

_____

Draw a line from the word in column one to its definition in column two.

14. nectar   a. a measurement of the frequency of sound waves

15. predator   b. change to fit into a specific environment

16. hertz   c. an animal that hunts and eats other animals

17. heredity   d. a sweet substance that plants produce

18. coexist   e. to live in peace with one another

19. adapt   f. genes and traits that are passed from parent to child

Circle the letter of the best answer to each question below.

1. Heat is

    a. never present in cold substances.

    b. only found in a microwave oven.

    c. molecules not moving.

    d. energy on the move.

2. _____ moving through matter creates sound.

    a. Air

    b. Vibrations

    c. Electricity

    d. Magnetism

Write your answers on the lines below.

3. If the genes for both a dominant and a recessive trait are present in an individual, which trait will it have?

    _____

4. What are the two types of weathering?

    _____   _____

5. Why does weathering need to happen before erosion can occur?

    _____

6. Use an example from Chapters 1–3 to show how scientific knowledge is a group effort.

    _____

    _____

7. What are two steps you should always take before beginning an experiment?

    _____   _____

8. What two types of particles are found in every kind of atom?

    _____   _____

9. Light, radio waves, and microwaves are all part of the _____ spectrum.

10. The atomic number for aluminum is 13. How many of the following particles does each aluminum atom contain?

    Electrons: _____   Protons: _____

11. Why did wolves become endangered? Why were they reintroduced to Yellowstone National Park?

    _____

    _____

12. An animal that lives in the African savanna is in danger of becoming extinct. Make an argument for why it is important to save this animal.

    _____

    _____

13. Explain how atoms are different in a solid versus a liquid.

    _____

14. Why do bees and flowers need one another?

    _____

    _____

15. Some plants are pollinated by _____ instead of by insects or animals.

16. List two reasons that animals use echolocation.

    _____

Read each sentence below. Underline the correct answer from the two choices.

17. Scientists use (data, conclusions) to prove or disprove their ideas.

18. The (Kelvin, Celsius) temperature scale starts at absolute zero.

19. The Wright Brothers added a (propeller, rudder) to the tail of their flying machine.

20. Electricity is the movement of (protons, electrons) from one atom to another.

21. An ion is an atom with an electrical (charge, matter).

22. The highest point of a wave is the (trough, crest).

23. A child jumping rope is an example of (kinetic, potential) energy.

24. (Fraternal, Identical) twins are no more alike than any other pair of siblings.

25. The (central, autonomic) nervous system controls involuntary activities.

Lesson 4.1 — Keeping Time

What's the difference between the Jurassic and the Mesozoic periods?

Our planet's history covers a vast amount of time. Human history can often be discussed using exact years, but scientists need a different system for discussing **geological** time. Geologists divide time using a naming system. It begins with a broad category and gets more specific. Eons are the biggest blocks of time. Each eon lasts for about a billion years.

The first eon is the Hadean. It begins with Earth's formation 4.6 billion years ago and ends when life first appeared almost a billion years later. During the Hadean eon, Earth was a boiling stew of lava and steam.

The next eon is the Archean. Earth's surface finally cooled, and rocks began to solidify, forming the first land. Earth's first life forms appeared, too—mostly **bacteria** and a few other **microscopic** organisms.

The third eon is the Proterozoic. Earth's atmosphere filled with oxygen, and scientists think this helped early life forms **evolve**. By the time the Proterozoic ended 500 million years ago, the first **multi-cellular** organisms had appeared, and Earth was about to explode with life.

Eons are divided into smaller units called *eras*, and eras are divided into periods. The first period after the Proterozoic eon ended is called the *Cambrian*. This period is famous because life on Earth suddenly became much more **diverse**. Fossils show that about 50 new, complex life forms evolved during this period. Scientists named this important event the *Cambrian Explosion*.

The Cambrian period signals the start of the Paleozoic era. This era saw major changes in Earth's structures and life forms. Mountains formed when all the land drifted together into a supercontinent, called *Pangaea*. Life was found only in the oceans when the Paleozoic began, and the most complex animal was the trilobite—an extinct type of insect. By the end of this era, the first dinosaurs roamed the landscape, and seed-bearing plants spread across the planet.

The next era, the Mesozoic, is famous for being the age of dinosaurs. For almost 200 million years, these giant reptiles ruled Earth. About 65 million years ago, something caused them to become extinct. Mammals—including human beings—rose in their place to dominate the planet.

geological: having to do with geology, the science of Earth's history

bacteria: tiny, one-celled organisms

microscopic: too small to be seen without a microscope

evolve: to grow or change gradually, often into a more complex form

multi-cellular: made of more than one cell

diverse: differing from one another

Geologists divide periods into even smaller units called *epochs*.

Right now, we are living in the Phanerozoic eon, the Cenozoic era, the Neogene period, and the Holocene epoch.

Placing Earth's entire history into a 24-hour day makes it easier to see how long ago certain events happened—and just how recently other ones did. Beginning at 12:00 A.M., for example, the Cambrian Explosion didn't happen until 10:30 P.M., the age of dinosaurs lasted only from about 11:20 to 11:40 P.M., and human beings didn't arrive until 30 seconds before midnight.

Era	Precambrian	Paleozoic	Mesozoic	Cenozoic
Period		Cambrian 543–490 / Ordovician 490–443 / Silurian 443–417 / Devonian 417–354 / Carboniferous 354–290 (Mississippian 354–323, Pennsylvanian 323–290) / Permian 290–248	Triassic 248–206 / Jurassic 206–144 / Cretaceous 144–65	Tertiary 65–1.8 / Quaternary 1.8–Present

Beginning of Earth — 543 — 248 — 65 — Present

millions of years ago

Circle the letter of the best answer to each question below.

1. Which of the following is not a unit of geological time?

   a. period

   b. era

   c. dynasty

   d. epoch

2. Earth was formed about _____ years ago.

   a. 4.6 thousand

   b. 4.6 million

   c. 4.6 billion

   d. 4.6 trillion

3. The Mesozoic era is famous because it's when

   a. human beings first appeared.

   b. dinosaurs ruled the planet.

   c. trilobites became extinct.

   d. Earth was first formed.

Write your answers on the lines below.

4. Explain what the Cambrian Explosion was.

   _____

   _____

5. Why do you think scientists divide time into distinct categories?

   _____

   _____

Unifying Concepts and Processes

Look carefully at a globe or map of the world. Compare the shapes of the continents. What do you think led scientists to form the theory that all of Earth's land was once a single supercontinent?

_____

An Inside Look at Earth

subterranean: existing or working underground

radius: a length of measure from the center of a circle or sphere to its outer edge

geologists: scientists who study Earth

molten: melted by very great heat

As the plates in Earth's crust drift about, they bump and scrape against each other. Mountains form where the edges of two or more plates have crashed into each other.

Sometimes, the edge of one plate will slide underneath the edge of another plate. This doesn't happen smoothly, though. The plates press against each other with increasing pressure until, suddenly, one of them breaks free and lurches ahead, causing an earthquake.

What would you really find if you tried to dig a hole to China?

In 1864, Jules Verne published his now-famous adventure story *Journey to the Center of the Earth*. In the story, a professor and his nephew descend into a volcano and follow caves that lead them deep inside Earth. They see dinosaurs, giant insects, and massive mushrooms. They even sail across a **subterranean** ocean. Eventually, the travelers return to Earth's surface.

As exciting as Verne's story is, it's entirely fictional. Human beings could never survive a journey to Earth's center. The heat and pressure deep below Earth's surface are high enough to turn stone to liquid. In fact, the farthest below ground human beings have ever gone is just a little more than two miles. Earth's **radius** is 4,000 miles. If Earth were an apple, human beings have just barely started digging through the peel.

Geologists divide Earth's structure into three layers—the core, the mantle, and the crust. The crust is the outermost layer. It's also the thinnest. The most common element found in Earth's crust is oxygen, but this oxygen is not in a form you can breathe. Oxygen mixes with lots of other elements to form solid substances. These substances and others combine to form the rocks in Earth's crust. After oxygen, silicon is the most abundant element in the crust.

Earth's crust isn't the same thickness everywhere. Under the ocean, it's only about five miles thick, but on land it can reach 40 miles or more. The crust is broken up into giant pieces, called *plates*, which slowly move around the planet. They are floating on a massive layer of liquid rock found in Earth's mantle.

The mantle is the biggest part of Earth's structure. It's about 1,800 miles thick, and makes up about two-thirds of Earth's volume. The intense pressure found deep inside Earth creates incredible amounts of heat. Rocks that would be solids in the temperature range at Earth's surface change states and become liquids in the mantle.

The innermost part of Earth's structure is the core. It is made almost entirely of iron, so it is very dense. The core is divided into two sections—the inner core and the outer core. The inner core is solid iron, but it's surrounded by **molten** iron that makes up the outer core. The temperature at Earth's center is more than 9,000°F. If Jules Verne had known that, he might have thought twice about sending his characters there.

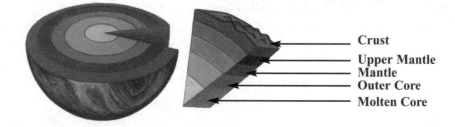

— Crust
— Upper Mantle
— Mantle
— Outer Core
— Molten Core

Circle the letter of the best answer to each question below.

1. Earth's crust is broken up into _____ that move around the planet.

   a. mantles

   b. layers

   c. plates

   d. radius

2. Earth's mantle

   a. is made mostly of iron.

   b. makes up nearly two-thirds of Earth's volume.

   c. is in Earth's center.

   d. All of the above

3. Where is molten rock found inside Earth?

   a. the inner core

   b. the outer core

   c. the mantle

   d. Both b and c

Write your answers on the lines below.

4. Explain why large pieces of Earth's crust move around and bump into each other.

   _____

   _____

5. Why do you think oxygen is the most abundant element in Earth's crust?

   _____

What's Next?

The four inner planets are called *terrestrial planets* because they are made mostly of rock. The four outer planets are called *gas giants* because they are made mostly of gases. Do the other planets in our solar system have crusts, mantles, and cores, too? Go to the library or look online and find what lies below the surfaces of other planets.

Recycled Air

fixed: steady and unchanging

oxygen cycle: the cycle that shows the movement of oxygen between the air, plants, and animals on Earth

photosynthesis: the process by which plants make their own food using light, water, and carbon dioxide

greenhouse gases: gases in the atmosphere that trap Earth's heat

Marine animals need oxygen to survive, too. They get their oxygen from water, which is made of hydrogen and oxygen (H_2O).

Without greenhouse gases, Earth's average temperature would be about 60°F colder. The greenhouse gases got their name because they work the same way a greenhouse for plants does—by trapping the heat of the sun.

"One acre of forest absorbs six tons of carbon dioxide and puts out four tons of oxygen. This is enough to meet the annual needs of 18 people."—U.S. Department of Agriculture

What's in the air you breathe?

Oxygen makes up about 21% of the air in Earth's atmosphere. It hasn't always been that way, though. When Earth was first formed, there was barely any oxygen in the atmosphere. Over billions of years, the amount of plant life on Earth increased. Plants produce oxygen, so its levels in the air increased, too.

Today, the amount of oxygen in the atmosphere is **fixed**, which means it is steady and doesn't change. This fixed amount of oxygen is constantly being used and produced by all living things on Earth. It's part of an ongoing cycle called the **oxygen cycle**.

Plants are the key to the oxygen cycle. Plants take in water, carbon dioxide from the air, and energy from the sun. They use these materials to make their own food. This process is called **photosynthesis**. During photosynthesis, oxygen molecules from the water are freed and can be released into the air.

Human beings and animals breathe in oxygen, which is necessary for survival. They exhale carbon dioxide, which can be later used by plants for photosynthesis, which produces more oxygen. See how the cycle keeps repeating itself? Plants actually use oxygen from the air, too. During photosynthesis, which needs light to take place, plants make and store food. Then, they use oxygen to turn the food they've stored into usable energy, just like human beings and animals do.

If plants use carbon dioxide, and there are plenty of plants on Earth, why is too much carbon dioxide in Earth's atmosphere a problem? Carbon dioxide is one of the **greenhouse gases**. These gases trap heat from Earth's surface. Greenhouse gases aren't a bad thing—without them it would be too cold on Earth for most living things to survive. The problem is that human activities have changed the amount of greenhouse gases in the atmosphere.

Burning fossil fuels, like coal and oil, produce greenhouse gases. Today, there are higher levels of them in the atmosphere than there have been in more than 400,000 years. They trap more of Earth's heat and are causing the planet to become warmer. This can cause flooding, changes in weather, and harmful changes in animals' habitats.

Circle the letter of the best answer to the question below.

1. Why are there more greenhouse gases in the atmosphere today?

   a. because the temperature on Earth has slowly been increasing

   b. because there are more plants on Earth today than there have ever been before

   c. because human beings burn a lot of fossil fuels

   d. Both b and c

Use the words in the box to complete the sentences below.

atmosphere	photosynthesis	cycle	greenhouse gases

2. Plants use water, carbon dioxide, and sunlight to make food in a process called _____.

3. _____ trap the heat from Earth.

4. A _____ is a pattern that repeats itself.

5. Oxygen is naturally found in Earth's _____.

Write your answers on the lines below.

6. Explain how greenhouse gases can be both good for life on Earth as well as harmful.

   _____

   _____

7. Would human and animal life on Earth be possible without plants? Explain.

   _____

8. Why do plants need oxygen?

   _____

Unifying Concepts and Processes

All kinds of cycles are important to life on Earth. Think of another natural cycle, and describe one way it is similar to the oxygen cycle.

_____

_____

vacant: empty, not filled

retain: keep; hold back

When a meteorologist says that a low-pressure system is in your area, you might soon see rain. Storm systems are carried along with the air currents. When you're in the low-pressure area, the currents are heading toward you, and if there's a storm around, they're bringing it right to you.

High pressure means nice weather, though, because the storm systems will be moving away.

The windiest place on Earth is the continent of Antarctica, which is the coldest and driest place, too. Wind speeds close to 200 miles per hour have been recorded there.

Why is air always moving around in Earth's atmosphere?

It's a sticky, hot summer afternoon. Suddenly, a cool breeze drifts over you. It's refreshing, but it only lasts a few seconds. Then, the air is still and warm again. Where did the breeze come from?

Wind is air in motion. Changes in the pressures and temperatures in Earth's atmosphere are what cause air currents to move. Pressure and temperature are different things, but they are closely related. The more pressure something is under, the higher temperature it will have. Pressure pushes the molecules in a substance closer together. They have less room to move around, so they begin bumping into each other with greater speed and energy. The faster molecules move, the higher the temperatures.

Areas under higher pressure always move toward areas with lower pressure. Think of the air trapped inside a tire. It's under a lot of pressure. When the valve is opened, the air rushes out toward the lower pressure outside the tire. On a much larger scale, this is what happens in Earth's atmosphere.

Air near Earth's surface is warmer—and under more pressure—than air higher up in the atmosphere. This warm air naturally rises upward, because air currents flow from areas of high pressure to areas of low pressure. When the warm air rises, though, air from someplace else near Earth's surface has to flow in to take its place. Air currents move sideways to fill the spaces left **vacant** by rising warm air.

Air is constantly on the move in Earth's atmosphere because the surface is never heated evenly. As the planet rotates, different areas get heated or cooled, depending on whether or not they face the sun. Some parts of Earth's surface also **retain** or lose heat more easily than others.

A good example is the constant breeze blowing at the beach. The ocean reflects a lot of sunlight, so the air above it stays cooler than air over land, which absorbs more of the sun's heat. The hot air on land rises into the Earth's cooler, upper atmosphere. The ocean air isn't as warm, so it doesn't move up into the atmosphere nearly as quickly as the air on land. Instead, the ocean air is pulled toward land in order to fill the space left vacant by the rising air. This creates a wind that blows from the ocean toward land and doesn't slow down until the sun sets.

Circle the letter of the best answer to each question below.

1. Which of the following is not a cause of wind?

    a. changes in temperature

    b. changes in pressure

    c. the moon's orbit

    d. Earth's rotation

2. Why is it always windy at the beach?

    a. The temperature on land is different from the temperature at sea.

    b. The air pressure on land is different from the pressure at sea.

    c. More of the sun's heat is absorbed by land than by water.

    d. All of the above

3. Warm air near Earth's surface usually

    a. rises into Earth's upper atmosphere.

    b. cools down when a good breeze blows by.

    c. follows cooler air out to sea.

    d. doesn't move.

Write your answers on the lines below.

4. Land doesn't hold heat as well as water does. Once the sun sets, the ocean still has heat to give off, but the land does not. This means the ocean air is warmer at night than the air over land. Which way does the breeze blow?

    _____

5. In your own words, explain why a high-pressure system usually means nice weather.

    _____

    _____

6. Because Earth is a sphere, the equator gets more of the sun's warmth than the poles. Which direction do air currents usually flow, toward the poles or away from the poles? Explain your answer.

    _____

    _____

Looking to the Skies

Ptolemaic system:
the theory that Earth
is at the center of the
universe

heliocentric: centered
around the sun

axis: an imaginary
line on which a planet
rotates

infinite: going on
forever; without end

Copernicus's ideas
were not accepted at
first. It would be
many years after his
death that the
telescope would be
invented and his ideas
could be observed and
tested. Even then,
political and religious
leaders rejected the
ideas because they
were different than
religious teachings
and ancient
philosophy. This may
be why Copernicus
didn't publish his
life's work until the
year he died. Today,
we know that
Copernicus's
heliocentric system
was the springboard
for modern
astronomy.

What can we learn from an astronomer who lived nearly 500 years ago?

For many years, scientists believed that Earth was located at the center of the universe and that the sun and the moon moved around it. The Greek astronomer and mathematician Ptolemy devised this **Ptolemaic system** in A.D. 150. It was considered scientific fact for more than 1,500 years. It's easy to see why people believed Ptolemy's idea. As they watched the sun and planets move, it appeared to them that Earth was standing still.

In 1543, Nicolaus Copernicus, one of the world's greatest thinkers, had an idea that the universe was **heliocentric**, or centered around the sun. His life's work, a book called *On the Revolutions of the Celestial Spheres*, is considered by many scholars to be the beginning of everything we understand about our universe today. His book was a turning point in the history of science. For the first time in ages, scientists began to question everything that their ancestors taught them about the natural world.

Using mathematics, Copernicus created a model that could answer many of the questions that bothered him about the Ptolemaic system. He wanted to prove that the sun, not Earth, was the center of our solar system.

Copernicus realized that Earth and the other planets in the solar system experienced three types of movements: revolution, rotation, and tilting. The planets orbit, or revolve in circles, around the sun. Copernicus also discovered that while orbiting the sun, planets rotated on their own axes. Earth's **axis** is an imaginary line drawn from the North Pole to the South Pole. As the planets rotated, they also tilted on their axes. The tilting of Earth created the seasons—spring, summer, fall, and winter.

Copernicus's theory also led to scientists' understanding that the universe is much bigger than they had thought. Astronomers did not yet know that our solar system didn't fill the entire universe. Eventually, they learned that Earth's solar system is just one of billions in the universe and that the universe is perhaps **infinite**. This idea was difficult for people to imagine at the time. Even today, scientists still debate the size of the universe.

Circle the letter of the best answer to each question below.

1. Earth's seasons are the result of

   a. the planet tilting on its axis as it rotates.

   b. Earth's position in the universe.

   c. Earth being at the center of the solar system.

   d. None of the above

2. Which of the following statements is true?

   a. Modern scientists have found that few of Copernicus's ideas were correct.

   b. Early astronomers believed that Earth stood still while the sun moved around it.

   c. Earth's movement around the sun takes 24 hours.

   d. Earth's axis and its equator are the same thing.

Write your answers on the lines below.

3. Explain how the Ptolemaic system was different from the heliocentric system.

   _____

   _____

4. What similarities do the movements of the planets share?

   _____

5. Why was the publication of Copernicus's book so important?

   _____

6. Why did it take so long for Copernicus's ideas to become widely accepted?

   _____

   _____

Unifying Concepts and Processes

Today, we know that Ptolemy's ideas about the movement of Earth, the planets, and the sun were incorrect. Explain why his ideas were still important to the development of Copernicus's theories. Do scientific theories always need to be correct to be useful?

_____

Not Just Planets

astronomers:
scientists who study astronomy, the science of objects in space

dwarf planet: a small, spherical planet that is not a satellite and has not absorbed all the objects that share its orbit around the sun

gravitational field: the area of gravity surrounding a planet that has an effect on other objects

For many years, Pluto was considered the ninth planet in our solar system. In 2005, an object larger than Pluto was discovered beyond the Kuiper Belt. Would it become the tenth planet? An international group of astronomers decided to create a new term for the smallest planets. Pluto, the newly found object, called *Eris*, and the large asteroid Ceres became known as our solar system's three dwarf planets.

What's the difference between a comet and an asteroid?

When our solar system first began, loose bits of rocks, gas, and dust orbited the sun. Eventually, this debris was pulled together by gravity, formed several huge clumps, and became the planets. Not every piece of rock or dust became part of a planet, though. Many of the smaller chunks are still making their way around the solar system today.

Asteroids are pieces of rock and metal that orbit the sun. They can be as small as specks of dust or as large as several miles wide. Nearly all asteroids are located between Mars and Jupiter in an area called the *asteroid belt*. **Astronomers** estimate that there are one million or more asteroids larger than half a mile wide hurtling along in the asteroid belt. It sounds like a crowded place, but the asteroids are spread out across such a huge area, it would be very difficult to hit one on accident.

The largest asteroid in the belt—and the first one ever discovered—is Ceres, a chunk of rock almost 600 miles wide. Today, Ceres is known as a **dwarf planet**.

Scientists think that the pieces of rock in the asteroid belt might have formed a planet, but because Jupiter's powerful **gravitational field** is nearby, the pieces were prevented from pulling together.

Centaurs are large chunks of frozen rock orbiting between Jupiter and Neptune. They were first discovered in the 1970s, and about 100 have been found so far. Centaurs are icy because they orbit so far from the sun's heat. The largest centaur, Chariklo, is about 140 miles wide. Much about centaurs is still unknown, but astronomers believe that they originally come from an area beyond Neptune called the *Kuiper Belt*.

About 35,000 objects have been found in the Kuiper Belt, but the largest and most famous one is the dwarf planet Pluto. Many of the objects in the Kuiper Belt travel around the sun in orbits that closely follow Neptune's path around the sun.

Comets are the loners of the solar system. Each one of these frozen chunks of rock and ice has its own unique orbit. A comet's orbit carries it far beyond the Kuiper Belt and then back toward the inner solar system. When comets approach the sun's heat and light, tails of gas and dust are lit up behind them. The comet zooms tightly around the sun before heading back out into the far reaches of the solar system.

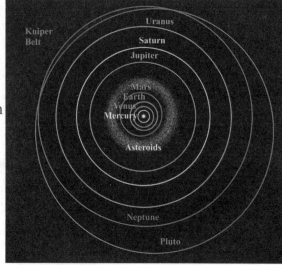

Circle the letter of the best answer to each question below.

1. The Kuiper Belt is

   a. another name for the asteroid belt.

   b. located beyond Neptune's orbit.

   c. filled with comets.

   d. Both a and b

2. Where are centaurs found?

   a. between Jupiter and Neptune

   b. in the Kuiper Belt

   c. orbiting dwarf planets

   d. in the asteroid belt

Write your answers on the lines below.

3. Even though there are more than a million asteroids in the asteroid belt, why doesn't NASA have any trouble sending spacecraft through it?

   _____

   _____

4. What do most scientists think prevented the rocks in the asteroid belt from forming into a planet?

   _____

5. What makes comets different from other rocks orbiting the sun?

   _____

6. Why is Pluto no longer considered one of the major planets in our solar system?

   _____

What's Next?

Natural satellites, or moons, orbit most of the planets in our solar system. The number and sizes of moons surrounding each planet vary greatly. For example, Earth has only one moon, but Saturn has more than 50. Which planet has the most moons? Which planets have no moons? Are any of the moons larger than planets?

Hubble's Galaxies

ellipses: ovals; shapes similar to flattened circles

nebulae: clouds of gas and dust that are where new stars form

The Milky Way galaxy is where our solar system is located. The Milky Way is a rotating, spiral galaxy. The sun and all of the objects surrounding it travel around the Milky Way's center once every 240 million years or so. Our galaxy contains about 300 billion stars and is about 100,000 light years in diameter.

It's hard to picture something as huge as a galaxy. If our entire solar system was just an inch in diameter, the Milky Way would be about 80 miles wide.

Is every light in the night sky a star?

On the clearest, darkest nights, the sky becomes filled with tiny points of light. Ancient astronomers grouped these shining dots into constellations. The familiar shapes helped human beings begin to map the stars. With the invention of the telescope, the tiny specks of light could be seen more clearly, and astronomers soon discovered that many stars had unusual shapes. Many of them were **ellipses**, spirals, and sometimes even irregularly shaped blobs. Were these things actually stars, or something else?

The early astronomers named these unusual objects **nebulae**. They knew that the visible stars in the night sky were members of the Milky Way galaxy, which also includes our sun. But they weren't sure if nebulae were part of the Milky Way, too. It wasn't until the 1920s that this mystery was solved.

The famous astronomer Edwin Hubble used the newly built Hooker Telescope—the most powerful telescope at the time—to make an amazing discovery. He could see that each nebula was actually made of many individual stars. Hubble also proved that nebulae were much too far away to be part of the Milky Way. With this information, he showed that the thousands of nebulae spread across the night sky were, in fact, thousands of galaxies, each one holding billions of stars. The universe was immensely bigger than anyone had ever imagined before.

Today, astronomers know that the universe contains billions of galaxies. They come in many different shapes and sizes. A very small galaxy may contain only about ten million stars, but a giant galaxy can hold as many as a trillion. Hubble devised a system for classifying galaxies by their shapes:

- Elliptical galaxies can be shaped like circles or ovals. The stars move about in random directions. Elliptical galaxies contain older stars, and there is very little gas or dust floating around in between them.

- Spiral galaxies contain many young stars that slowly rotate around a central point. Star-filled arms swirl out from the galaxy's center. Astronomers believe most spiral galaxies have black holes at their centers. These galaxies also contain a lot of gas and dust, which gravity compresses to form new stars.

- Irregular galaxies are those that aren't shaped like either ellipses or spirals. Sometimes, galaxies collide and become oddly shaped, or gravity from another galaxy causes the irregular shape.

Circle the letter of the best answer to each question below.

1. The universe contains _____ of galaxies.

   a. hundreds

   b. millions

   c. billions

   d. trillions

2. Irregular galaxies are shaped like

   a. circles.

   b. ellipses.

   c. spirals.

   d. None of the above

3. Our sun is a star in the

   a. Nebula galaxy.

   b. Andromeda galaxy.

   c. Milky Way galaxy.

   d. Hubble galaxy.

Write your answers on the lines below.

4. Why couldn't early astronomers tell the difference between single stars and entire galaxies when they looked at the night sky?

   _____

5. What are the two important discoveries Hubble made that proved other galaxies exist outside our own?

   _____

   _____

6. Explain how the meaning of the word *nebula* is different today than it was before Hubble's discoveries.

   _____

   _____

Circle the letter of the best answer to each question below.

1. What are centaurs?

   a. frozen rocks orbiting between Jupiter and Neptune

   b. large rocks orbiting in the asteroid belt

   c. dwarf planets found in the Kuiper Belt

   d. small moons orbiting Jupiter

2. What was Pangaea?

   a. the first type of dinosaur

   b. an ancient ocean

   c. a supercontinent that contained all of Earth's land

   d. a mountain range formed by Earth's first volcanoes

3. Earth's structure is divided into three main layers: the crust, the _____, and the core.

   a. plates

   b. molten

   c. mantle

   d. radius

4. Warm air near Earth's surface usually

   a. blows to the south.

   b. gets pulled toward the equator.

   c. moves rapidly toward large bodies of water.

   d. rises into the upper atmosphere.

Write your answers on the lines below.

5. What major change occurred during the Cambrian Explosion?

   _____

6. What is the most abundant element in Earth's crust? _____

7. Why do Earth's plates move?

   _____

8. Explain Earth's oxygen cycle.

_____

_____

9. Why are too many greenhouse gases in Earth's atmosphere harmful to the environment?

_____

10. How were Copernicus's ideas different from the ideas of earlier astronomers?

_____

11. Many scientists believe Jupiter had an effect on the asteroid belt. What was it?

_____

12. Why is Pluto no longer considered a planet? What is it considered today?

_____

_____

13. What two important discoveries were made by Edwin Hubble using the Hooker Telescope?

_____

14. The three main types of galaxies are _____, elliptical, and irregular.

Write **true** or **false** next to each statement below.

15. _____ Human beings evolved about a million years after dinosaurs became extinct.

16. _____ Earth is the only planet that rotates on its axis.

17. _____ The Milky Way Galaxy contains our solar system.

18. _____ Copernicus's ideas were not widely accepted until years after his death.

19. _____ The asteroid belt contains a million rocks larger than half a mile each.

20. _____ Everything in the universe revolves around the sun.

21. _____ Earth's crust is much thinner underneath the oceans than on land.

22. _____ Areas of high pressure always move toward areas of low pressure.

Lesson 5.1 When the Ground Moves

seismogram: a recording of the ground's motion at a specific time

pendulum: a heavy weight hanging free from a fixed position

stylus: a writing utensil, like a pen, that records the information of a shaking seismograph

seismic waves: waves that travel through Earth from the center of an earthquake

Around A.D. 132, Chinese scientist Chang Heng invented the first seismograph. Heng's invention was called the *dragon jar*. At the top of the jar, eight dragon heads sat on the brim with balls in their mouths. At the bottom of the jar were eight frogs, each directly under a dragon head. When an earthquake happened, a ball dropped from a dragon's mouth into a frog's mouth. The dropped ball was said to face the direction of the earthquake.

Why do we need to know exactly where an earthquake starts?

On April 18, 1906, the ground violently shook from California to Oregon. Not only did the Great San Francisco earthquake shake the ground, it also started fires, destroyed buildings, and took lives. Scientists gathered information about this enormous earthquake, hoping to learn more about why earthquakes happen and whether there is a way to predict them.

One way that scientists studied the Great San Francisco earthquake was with data gathered from seismographs. A seismograph creates a chart called a **seismogram**, which is a record of the earth's motion at a specific time. The seismograph has a base that sits firmly in the ground and a heavy weight above called a **pendulum** that hangs from a string. When an earthquake causes the ground to move, the base of the seismograph moves, too. The weight stays still because the string that it hangs from absorbs all the movement. As the base moves below the motionless weight, the seismograph records the difference in position between the base and the weight.

In older seismographs, a writing utensil called a **stylus** is attached to the weight. When the base of the seismograph shakes, the stylus makes marks on a roll of paper. Today, many seismographs are digital. A computer records an earthquake's **seismic waves**, and then a printer prints out a seismogram.

Seismographic stations have been operating throughout the world for about 100 years. The main use of seismograph networks is to pinpoint the location of earthquakes. Although it's possible to find the general location of an earthquake from one station, it's more accurate to use three or more stations. When an earthquake happens, the surrounding seismographs send data to a central research center, where the seismograms are analyzed. Scientists can then determine where the earthquake occurred.

Seismograms are like fingerprints of earthquakes with patterns that can be matched and decoded. Seismograms can even be broken into smaller pieces. Scientists can then use computers to search for matching patterns among the pieces of all recorded seismograms.

Comparing earthquakes creates a better picture of Earth's plates and their constant motion. Even though scientists can't predict when an earthquake will happen, the more information they gather, the better they can predict where quakes will happen. With this information, safer roads and buildings can be designed in areas that are at high risk for earthquakes.

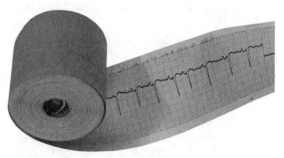

Circle the letter of the best answer to each question below.

1. What is a similarity between Heng's seismograph and a modern seismograph?

   a. Both use a stylus.

   b. Both produce a seismogram.

   c. Both can predict the exact time an earthquake will occur.

   d. The purpose of both is to find the location of an earthquake.

2. When an earthquake strikes, the _____ of a seismograph moves with the trembling ground.

   a. base

   b. pendulum

   c. seismogram

   d. stylus

Use the words in the box to complete the sentences below.

accurate	seismograph	patterns	pendulum

3. The weight used in a seismograph is called a _____.

4. Using several seismographic stations to locate the source of an earthquake provides more

   _____ results.

5. Scientists search for _____ when they analyze seismograms.

6. A _____ is a tool that helps scientists learn more about earthquakes.

Write your answers on the lines below.

7. Why does a seismograph's pendulum remain still during an earthquake?

   _____

8. If scientists can't predict when earthquakes will happen, why do they still study these natural events?

   _____

9. How is the exact location of an earthquake determined?

   _____

Super Foods

selective breeding:
the breeding of plants that have certain desirable characteristics

resistant: able to stand up against or fight against a force

genetically modified: the changing of an organism by the introduction of genes that it did not naturally possess

One problem with GM foods is that there is no good way to keep them contained. Seeds and pollen can drift into neighboring fields or be carried there by insects and animals.

In the United States, GM foods don't need to be labeled the way they do in Europe. Organic foods in the U.S. often have labels saying they do not contain GM foods. This is a hard claim to make, though, since GM crops can't really be completely contained.

How do you feel about eating a food whose genes were altered by scientists?

For hundreds of years, farmers have used a process called **selective breeding**. They found that some plants in a crop withstood disease and insects better than others. For their next crop, they would sow seeds only from the plants that were **resistant** to the insect. Over time, they bred plants that could resist many types of diseases and pests.

In the 1980s, a new technology was born. Instead of spending years and years breeding plants to get certain traits, scientists had found a shortcut. They were able to add genes to the plants. This allowed them to quickly create plants that could live through times of drought. They could also make crops that wouldn't be destroyed by fungus or eaten by insects. What was even more amazing was that they could use genes from other species—something that couldn't be done with selective breeding.

Before any of these **genetically modified** (GM) crops could be used to provide food for human beings, the FDA had to approve them. This happened in the mid-1990s, but the first products weren't a success. A breakthrough came when soybeans were genetically modified. A popular type of weed-killer could be applied to this new type of soybean crop. It would kill weeds, but it wouldn't kill the soybeans.

Creating GM crops sounds like a perfect solution to a lot of problems. Farmers can make more money because they lose fewer plants. They're also able to produce more fruits and vegetables. Some crops are bred to contain extra vitamins and nutrition. Others can help people fight illness. These advances might even help fight hunger and disease around the world.

Not everyone thinks that GM foods are a good idea, though. Some people are worried that there are health risks to eating foods that weren't created using natural methods. There is also the problem of "superweeds"—weeds that evolve over time and become resistant to weed-killers. Another problem is the effect that changing a plant's genetic make-up can have on insects. You've already learned how connected the different pieces of nature are. A change in the plants might kill some insects. It can also result in other insects evolving into "superinsects" that are resistant to pest control.

Genetically modified foods have become a part of modern society. Many people have strong feelings about them, one way or the other. Where do you stand on this controversial issue?

Circle the letter of the best answer to the question below.

1. Which of the following statements is not true?

   a. Genetically modifying foods is a quicker process than selective breeding.

   b. Soybeans were the first GM crop to become widely used.

   c. GM foods do not need to be labeled anywhere in the world.

   d. Not everyone agrees about whether GM foods are safe for people and the environment.

Write your answers on the lines below.

2. Give three examples of traits that scientists might give a fruit or vegetable plant.

   _____

   _____

3. Explain how selective breeding is different from genetically modifying a crop. How is it similar?

   _____

   _____

   _____

4. Why can't GM crops be contained?

   _____

5. Do you think it's a good idea for scientists to create genetically modified crops? Explain your answer.

   _____

   _____

Unifying Concepts and Processes

Imagine that a large farm grows corn that is resistant to a certain type of insect. What effect do you think this would have on that insect? Do you think it would have any effects on the food chain? Explain.

_____

_____

_____

Sharp as a Laser

concentrated: gathered into one area or space

beam: a stream of waves or particles of light or energy

wavelength: the distance between two crests in a wave; used to measure the different types of electromagnetic waves in the spectrum

amplified: increased in strength

precise: very exact

The letters in the word *laser* stand for "light amplification by stimulated emission of radiation."

The first lasers used microwaves, so they were called *masers*.

Always be careful around lasers. You never want to look directly at a laser beam or have one pointed into your eye. All laser beams contain waves of energy that have been concentrated into a narrow stream. Even cool laser beams, like those used in CDs or bar code scanners, can damage the sensitive cells at the back of your eyeball.

How are lasers used as tools in medicine?

Lasers streaking across space are common sights in science fiction movies. In real life, lasers are put to use for much more helpful tasks. They decode the information stored in CDs, DVDs, and bar codes. They are used to cut through metal and fabric. The use of lasers in medicine, though, may be one of their most important jobs.

A laser creates a powerful, **concentrated beam** of light. Have you ever used a magnifying glass on a sunny day? Sunlight passing through the lens becomes focused onto one tiny spot. The concentrated sunlight contains enough heat to start a fire. Lasers don't work exactly like that, but the idea is similar.

Remember, light is electromagnetic radiation, a kind of energy that moves in waves. Every color you see is a different **wavelength** of light. White light is all the wavelengths of color combined. The white light from a bulb is all the different wavelengths spreading out in every direction. The light coming from a laser, though, is one wavelength concentrated into a narrow beam.

Inside a laser, there are two mirrors facing each other. Light bounces back and forth between the mirrors and becomes **amplified**. The waves of energy that leave the laser are powerful, and they can be aimed at very specific targets. Some lasers use this energy to create intense heat that can burn through materials like metal.

Today, lasers are common medical tools because they are **precise** and clean. A doctor can aim a laser beam at something as small as a single cell or cut through just a single layer of skin. Lasers are also very clean tools because nothing but light touches the patient. A scalpel or other metal cutting tool can carry bacteria or other germs.

Lasers that burn as they cut can prevent bleeding, too. The burnt tissue surrounding the cut gets cauterized, which means the blood vessels in it are sealed up.

Not all lasers use heat to make their cuts. The lasers used in eye surgery would damage the delicate tissues in the eyeball if they created too much heat. Instead of burning their way through the tissue, the waves of energy in these laser beams break up molecules, and the atoms just float away. A clean, precise cut is made without any heat.

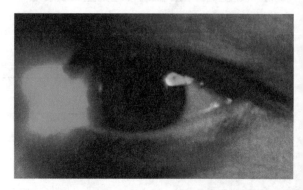

Circle the letter of the best answer to each question below.

1. A laser creates a beam of

    a. light.

    b. electromagnetic radiation.

    c. energy.

    d. All of the above

2. Which of the following statements is not true?

    a. Lasers emit waves of energy.

    b. All laser beams are dangerous because they are hot.

    c. A laser beam contains waves of only one length.

    d. White light contains every other color of light.

Write your answers on the lines below.

3. Review the selection. In your own words, explain how a laser beam is different from the light a light bulb produces.

    _____

    _____

4. Give two reasons why lasers are good surgical tools.

    _____

    _____

5. Do you think laser beams occur in nature? Why or why not?

    _____

    _____

What's Next?

One common use of lasers is to measure distance. The time it takes a beam of light to reflect off an object and then return to the laser tells how far away the object is. The astronauts of the Apollo missions placed reflectors on the lunar surface. They wanted to see if lasers could be used to find the exact distance from Earth to the moon. Find out whether this experiment worked, and if so, how far it is to the moon.

The Dawn of the Information Age

information: knowledge that can be shared

Babylonians: people of Babylon, a civilization that existed 4,000 years ago in the area that is now Iraq

characters: symbols used in writing and printing

efficient: capable of working without wasted effort or expense

text: the words and punctuation on a printed page

type: a rectangular piece of metal with a raised letter, number, or punctuation mark

The modern world begins with the Renaissance. This period of history saw a major change in how human beings looked at the world. Education, science, the arts, and the rights of individuals became important parts of society. The Renaissance began in Italy during the 1300s, but after Gutenberg invented his press, the ideas spread quickly across Europe.

Is there really such a thing as too much information?

Today, we live in a society filled with **information**. Just walk into a library or go online and you can find the answers to millions of questions you might have about the world. It hasn't always been so easy. Books used to be rare objects that only the wealthiest people in the world could afford to own. Every letter and punctuation mark was written by hand. A craftsperson could spend a year or more working carefully to produce just a single book. Around 1450, an invention created by Johannes Gutenberg decreased the amount of time it took information to spread through society.

Printing was around long before Gutenberg arrived. The ancient **Babylonians** had made stamps out of molded clay and carved stone. Many different cultures had used blocks and ink to stamp designs onto cloth. Chinese scholars had even carved individual **characters** out of wooden blocks. They used the blocks to print thousands of pages of religious materials. A similar printing method was used in Korea as well. This method of printing wasn't very practical, though. The Western alphabet has only 26 characters, but the Chinese and Korean languages have thousands. That's a lot of blocks to have on hand.

Gutenberg figured out a way to combine some of the different methods of printing he knew about. He saw that printing was most **efficient** when the individual characters could be moved around. He made tiny metal stamps for each letter and punctuation mark. The pieces were then arranged inside trays to spell out the **text** needed for each page. Ink was rolled across the characters, and then a piece of paper was laid across the top. A lever pulled down a flat piece of wood that pressed the paper against the ink to print a page of text. Gutenberg's press had six trays, so it could print six different pages at one time.

Although the alphabet has only 26 letters, Gutenberg still needed thousands of individual pieces of **type** in order to print six pages of text. Gutenberg and his assistants spent many hours arranging and inking all those letters. Making a book was still a lot of work—and each book was still expensive—but Gutenberg's press produced books in a lot less time and for less money than had ever been possible. Within a few short years, printing presses were up and running all over Europe and knowledge was being shared like never before.

Circle the letter of the best answer to each question below.

1. What did Johannes Gutenberg invent?

    a. carved wooden blocks used for printing

    b. an efficient printing press

    c. a new way to roll ink onto type

    d. All of the above

2. Why didn't printed text become widespread in China or Korea?

    a. They didn't have good inks.

    b. The wooden blocks were difficult to carve.

    c. Their written languages used thousands of characters.

    d. Neither language used punctuation.

3. Why is Gutenberg's machine called a *press*?

    a. because it was used to make newspapers

    b. because the paper was pressed against the ink

    c. because a button was pressed to make the machine work

    d. because the inks were made from pressed flowers

Write your answer on the lines below.

4. Explain why Gutenberg still needed thousands of pieces of type, even though the alphabet contains only 26 letters.

    _____

    _____

Unifying Concepts and Processes

Explain why the invention of the printing press had a powerful impact on the world of science. Do you think the Internet is having a similar effect today? Why or why not?

_____

_____

_____

satellites: any objects that orbit another object

space debris: human-made objects that orbit Earth and are no longer useful

Global Positioning System: technology used by a receiver that can determine its own location anywhere in the world within a few feet

After World War II, the United States and Russia were both serious about space exploration. This was a tense period in world history, and the rivalry over space travel was fierce. In 1955, the U.S. announced its plans to launch a satellite into space by spring of 1958. Two days later, the Soviet Union announced plans to launch its satellite six months sooner. On October 4, 1957, the Soviet Union successfully launched *Sputnik I*, the first artificial satellite, into space. The space race had officially begun.

How do scientists watch Earth without ever leaving the ground?

When we look up into the sky, we can't see the approximately 560 human-made **satellites** orbiting Earth. They are there, though, collecting information about our planet. Without these satellites, we couldn't make cell phone calls or monitor changes to the ozone layer.

Satellites can be spacecraft made on Earth and sent into space on a launch vehicle. They can be natural, too, like the moons that orbit planets. Sometimes, satellites are **space debris**.

Human-made satellites gather useful information. They orbit Earth at different altitudes and in different paths. Satellites are grouped according to their missions.

- Scientific research satellites gather information about the conditions of outer space. They also record changes on Earth and in its atmosphere and observe planets, stars, and other distant objects.

- Weather satellites measure cloud cover, temperature, air pressure, precipitation, and other conditions in the atmosphere. Weather sites on the Internet often post images sent back by these satellites.

- Communications satellites serve as relay stations, receiving radio signals from one place and sending them to another. A communications satellite can relay several TV programs or thousands of telephone calls at once.

- Navigation satellites allow hikers, as well as operators of aircraft, ships, and land vehicles to determine their exact locations. The satellites send a signal that is received by a vehicle or handheld device. This is called *GPS*, or **Global Positioning System** technology.

- Earth-observing satellites take special pictures to map and monitor Earth's resources. They are also used to find mineral deposits, to identify and study pollution, and to detect disease in crops and forests.

- The military uses all of these types of satellites. Some military satellites, often called *spy satellites*, can detect the launch of missiles, the course of ships at sea, and the movement of military equipment on the ground.

If equipment on a satellite stops working, operators on the ground will keep it running as long as it still provides some useful information. If not, they can shut it off. A satellite will then continue its orbit until it eventually slows down, falls back toward Earth, and burns up in the atmosphere.

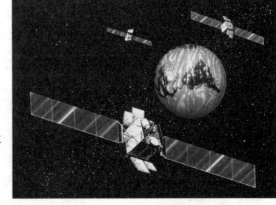

Write **true** or **false** next to each statement below.

1. _____ Cell phones and TV broadcasts rely on communications satellites.

2. _____ The United States was the first country to launch an artificial satellite.

3. _____ All satellites orbit Earth at the same altitude.

4. _____ Some of Earth's satellites are space debris.

Write your answers on the lines below.

5. What kind of satellite would most likely be used to gather information about the effects of pollution in South American rain forests?

_____

6. What is an example of a naturally occurring satellite?

_____

7. What happens to a satellite that is no longer working or no longer needed?

_____

8. List one similarity and one difference between natural satellites and human-made satellites.

_____

_____

9. How does a GPS work?

_____

10. What role did a satellite play in the beginning of the space race?

_____

11. Why would a satellite be a useful way for the military to gather information?

_____

_____

_____

The Birth of Photography

camera obscura: a Latin phrase that means *dark chamber*

projected: made to appear on a surface

exposed: made open or unprotected; allowed light to reach something

negative: having light and dark parts that appear opposite from how they look in real life

positive: having light and dark parts that appear the same as they do in real life

celluloid: a tough type of plastic; thin strips of celluloid are coated in light-sensitive chemicals to create film

People seldom smiled in early photos because they had to sit still for such a long time while the picture was being taken.

Digital cameras don't use film and chemicals. Instead, the image entering the camera falls onto a plate covered with tiny, light-sensitive electrical devices. They record the image in digital code and store the information on a removable computer disk.

Were cameras invented by just one person?

The path to photography began two thousand years ago in ancient Greece when Aristotle and Euclid described the idea of the **camera obscura**. This simple device was a box with a small hole in one side. When light entered the dark box through the hole, it **projected** an image against the opposite side.

By the 16th century, a lens was added to the camera. Still, the only way to preserve the image inside a camera obscura was to trace it by hand. Then, in 1724, Johann Schultz discovered a silver and chalk mixture that darkened when it was **exposed** to light. One hundred years later, Louis Daguerre and Joseph Niépce used this chemical mixture to create the first photographs.

They spread the mixture onto a copper plate and then placed the plate inside a camera obscura. The image that was projected onto the plate made the chemicals darken. The stronger the light was in the image, the darker the chemicals became. This meant the men ended up with a **negative** image. In order to get a **positive** image, they added mercury fumes to the plate. The shiny element stuck to the dark areas, which formed the first photographs.

Daguerre and Niépce's process was slow—it took several minutes to get a good image—but their *daguerreotypes* became popular during the 1800s. One big problem was that the chemicals were easily wiped away, and they would even react with other chemicals in the air. A daguerreotype had to be sealed inside a glass box to preserve its image. The chemicals were also dangerous for the photographers to handle.

As the 1800s progressed, better chemicals were found that made longer-lasting and less delicate photographs. Expensive copper plates were replaced, first by glass and then by paper. Finally, **celluloid** film that was precoated with dry chemicals became the safest and most popular choice.

By the end of the century, George Eastman's box cameras were being sold around the country. Each camera held enough celluloid film to take about 100 pictures. The film could be mailed to Eastman's company, where the pictures were developed and returned to the customer. Suddenly, anyone could take pictures, and cameras became common household devices.

Circle the letter of the best answer to the question below.

1. The earliest photographers had to be very careful because

   a. it was dangerous working in the dark.

   b. they handled poisonous chemicals.

   c. the cameras were big and heavy.

   d. their eyes could be damaged by light.

Write your answers on the lines below.

2. Explain why Eastman's box cameras allowed anyone to be a photographer.

   _____

   _____

3. Give two reasons why you think celluloid film replaced copper, glass, and paper plates.

   _____

   _____

4. All cameras use parts to carefully control the amount of light that gets inside. Why is controlling light important in photography?

   _____

5. Describe one difference between traditional cameras and digital cameras.

   _____

6. Describe one similarity between traditional cameras and digital cameras.

   _____

What's Next?

This selection mentions only five people from the history of photography, but there were many others who weren't mentioned. For example, William Fox Talbot made an important contribution to photography in the 1840s. What was it? When were the first color photographs taken? Who was Sergey Prokudin-Gorsky?

Everywhere You Go

saturated: filled completely

rigid: stiff and unmoving; not flexible

asphalt: a black material made from petroleum that is used for paving roads

The earliest paved roads were thought to have been built around 4000 B.C. Streets paved with stones have been found in Middle Eastern cities. Streets paved with logs have been found in England.

The Pan-American Highway is a network of roads that stretches from Alaska to South America and passes through more than a dozen countries.

At the peak of the Roman Empire, there were more than 53,000 miles of roads. The Appian Way (pictured) was built in 312 B.C. It was the main route to Greece and ran more than 350 miles. Parts of the road are still in use today.

What materials are used to construct roads?

Roads are something you use every day but probably don't spend much time thinking about. Without a good system of roads, it would be difficult to travel to places like school or work. Food and other products couldn't be transported to nearby stores. Emergency workers couldn't quickly reach a home on fire or a person in crisis. In one way or another, roads affect almost every single part of our lives.

A road is a pathway used by people, animals, or vehicles to get from one place to another. People needed a way to transport food and goods from place to place, so they began creating trails from the places they hunted or harvested to the places they lived. When the wheel was invented, there was a need for stronger, better roads. A road that was made only of dirt could become muddy or flooded in times of rain. Wheels could form ruts in the ground that made the roads difficult to use.

Today, most roads have three layers. The bottom layer is called the *road bed*. It is frequently made of soil, which is smoothed and leveled by bulldozers. The base course is the next level. It is often made of soil mixed with gravel, which is then flattened. This layer contains drainage pipes that keep the road from collapsing when the ground below is **saturated** with water.

The top layer is called the *wearing course* and must be very strong since it is in direct contact with traffic and the effects of weather. This layer may be made of a **rigid** material, like concrete, or flexible pavement, like **asphalt**. Each one has its advantages. It is cheaper and easier to build and repair an asphalt road, but a concrete road lasts longer and doesn't need as much maintenance. A road built of asphalt has a little give to it, which allows it to stand up to changes in weather and temperature. Concrete roads must often be built with metal rods to connect the slabs of concrete. Sometimes, metal bars or mesh are imbedded in the concrete to help keep it from cracking and to hold it together when it does.

The next time you're going somewhere, pay attention to the types of roads you travel over. Can you tell which materials were used to create them? Do they vary depending on their location and use? You might surprise yourself with how much you know about their construction.

Write your answers on the lines below.

1. What problem did the use of paved roads solve?

    _____

2. What two things create the greatest wear on a road?

    _____   _____

3. What is one advantage of using asphalt and one advantage of using concrete as the wearing course
    of a road?

    _____

    _____

4. Why do roads need to have good drainage systems?

    _____

5. The Roman Empire was one of history's biggest, most powerful, and longest-lasting empires. The
    Roman roads played an important role in the empire's success. Why?

    _____

    _____

6. What is the purpose of using metal bars or mesh in the construction of concrete roads?

    _____

7. Do you think the invention of cars had any effect on the number or types of roads that existed?
    Explain.

    _____

    _____

What's Next?

Did you know that recycled glass is being used in roads? Do some research at the library or online to
find out what other kinds of recycled materials are being used in building roads.

Circle the letter of the best answer to each question below.

1. Seismographs record information about

   a. wind.

   b. earthquakes.

   c. waves in the ocean.

   d. tornadoes.

2. Why is it hard for companies to say that their products don't contain any GM foods?

   a. because not all farmers tell the companies that they grow GM crops

   b. because some GM seeds aren't correctly labeled

   c. because pollen from GM crops can spread to the crops in other fields

   d. because companies don't always know what ingredients their foods contain

3. Why could anyone be a photographer using Eastman's box cameras?

   a. The Eastman Company developed the film.

   b. People didn't need special equipment or dangerous chemicals.

   c. The box cameras contained inexpensive celluloid film.

   d. All of the above

Write your answers on the lines below.

4. What's the most accurate way to find the location of an earthquake?

   _____

5. What is one benefit and one risk to genetically modifying crops?

   _____

   _____

6. Why are lasers useful medical tools?

   _____

7. Explain how a laser used for eye surgery is different from a laser used to cut metal.

   _____

8. What made Gutenberg's method of printing more efficient than other methods?

_____

9. What effect did Gutenberg's press have on society?

_____

10. What are two different kinds of satellites and how are they each used?

_____

_____

11. An astronaut working on the outside of the shuttle loses a small bolt, and it drifts off to begin orbiting Earth. Is the bolt a satellite, and if so, what kind?

_____

12. Why did other photography methods replace daguerreotypes?

_____

13. Why are drainage pipes placed beneath roads?

_____

14. Why did the use of wheeled vehicles change the way roads were built?

_____

Use the words in the box to complete the sentences below.

celluloid	asphalt	wavelength	atmosphere	type	seismic waves

15. During an earthquake, _____ move through the ground, causing it to shake.

16. Gutenberg's press used thousands of pieces of _____.

17. Every color of light has a different _____.

18. Copper and glass plates were replaced by _____ film that was less expensive.

19. Satellites that are no longer in use eventually reenter Earth's _____ and burn up.

20. _____ is a petroleum product that is used to pave roads.

Lesson 6.1 Cleaning Up

hygiene: the practice of keeping one's body clean and well-cared for

plague: a deadly illness carried by bacteria

The largest public Roman baths could hold as many as 3,000 bathers.

The ancient Egyptians had a recipe for toothpaste that used rock salt, mint, dried iris flowers, and crushed pepper. The first modern-looking toothbrush was invented in 1780. The handle was made of bone, and tufts of animal bristles poked out from small holes that had been drilled through it. Before its invention, people used things like twigs and feathers to clean their teeth.

"Hand-washing is the single most important means of preventing the spread of infection."—U.S. Centers for Disease Control

How has personal hygiene changed over the years?

What did you do when you got up this morning? After you used the bathroom, you probably washed your hands and brushed your teeth. You might have showered, brushed your hair, and put on clean clothes. Personal **hygiene** is a matter of habit. In some ways, this has always been true; it's just that habits were different in various times and places around the world.

For the early Greeks and Romans, baths were an important part of life. Large, public baths, which the Romans called *thermae*, were located in urban areas. These pool-like baths were a place for people to clean themselves, but they were also social meeting spaces.

During the Renaissance, diseases like the **plague** wiped out large populations. People were frightened and came to believe that water could make them ill. In a way, they were correct—if they drank dirty or contaminated water, they could become ill. However, some believed that bathing in water could also make them sick. As a result, they usually cleaned themselves by rubbing a dry towel over the parts of their bodies that weren't covered by clothing. As you can imagine, this didn't get them very clean!

Chamber pots and outhouses were a major reason why the water supply was dirty. They were often emptied into the streets, alleys, and waterways. Not only did this create strong odors, it also contaminated the water and caused illness. The creation of sewage systems that carried away waste led to a sharp decrease in sickness. It also made life in cities more bearable, especially in summer.

One of the biggest advances in personal hygiene came when the importance of hand-washing became known. During the 1840s, an Austrian doctor named Ignaz Semmelweis noticed that lots of women were dying after childbirth. He discovered that the medical students were carrying infections to the women from people who were ill or who had died. He had the students wash their hands in a special solution, and the women stopped dying. This sounds like an obvious solution, but it would be years before the knowledge of germs and how they carry disease was widely accepted.

Hygiene is both a personal and a public matter. It can help individuals stay healthy and feel good about themselves, and it can also stop the spread of illness. Even today, many habits vary by country. Travel to another part of the world and you might be surprised to see both similarities and differences in habits of personal hygiene.

Circle the letter of the best answer to each question below.

1. Which of the following is not an element of oral hygiene?

   a. regular dentist appointments

   b. dental floss

   c. toothpaste

   d. lipstick

2. The creation of sewage systems

   a. did not happen until after the invention of the modern toilet.

   b. helped stopped the spread of disease.

   c. kept a city's water supply clean.

   d. Both b and c

Write your answers on the lines below.

3. What was the purpose of the Roman *thermae*?

   _____

4. How did people clean themselves during the Renaissance when they were worried about water being contaminated?

   _____

5. Why is good personal hygiene important for both an individual and a community?

   _____

   _____

6. What life-saving connection did Dr. Semmelweis make by observing the medical practices at his hospital?

   _____

   _____

7. Why is hand-washing so important in stopping illnesses from spreading?

   _____

Safe Surfing

etiquette: social rules

censors: people or groups who examine material for inappropriate content

virus protection: a program that protects a computer from viruses that can damage it

virus: a hidden computer program that makes copies of itself and destroys or damages files

cite: to quote or show proof of

It's easy to type a message and send it without thinking about it. Once you've sent a message, though, you can't take it back. That's why you should always double-check that you haven't written anything you don't really mean or anything that could be misunderstood. When you speak to someone, the expression on your face and the tone of your voice sends a message along with your words. There aren't any cues like this in e-mails, so you need to choose your words carefully.

Do you know what safety rules to follow when you use the Internet?

The Internet is a powerful tool. With it, you can instantly send messages to someone who lives anywhere in the world. In just moments, you can access more information than could fill hundreds of libraries. As useful as it is, there are risks to using the Internet. The guidelines below can help you have fun, use proper **etiquette**, and stay safe online.

- Don't give out your personal information. It's fine to use your first name, but don't give anyone your last name, address, or phone number or tell them what school you attend. If you think there is a good reason to give out this information, check with a trusted adult first.

- The Internet can be a good place to connect with kids who have similar interests. You can talk about your shared hobbies online, but you shouldn't agree to meet with someone you've met on the Web. There's not really a good way to make sure that people are who they say they are online.

- If anything ever makes you uncomfortable while you're on the Web, let an adult know right away. There are no **censors** online, so it can be easy to come across inappropriate material.

- Passwords are meant to protect your privacy. Don't share them with anyone except your parents.

- Have you ever wanted to download a program or some software you found online? E-mails can also come with attachments to download. Check with an adult before you do this, and make sure your computer has **virus protection**. If it doesn't, a **virus** can infect your computer and cause all kinds of damage.

- When you e-mail or instant message (IM) your friends, it's common to use familiar language and abbreviations, like LOL for "laughing out loud" or TTYL for "talk to you later." Remember to consider who your audience is. If you are writing to an adult or someone you don't know well, use more formal, respectful language.

- The Internet is a terrific resource for researching papers or projects for school. Anyone can post material online, though, so be sure you use only trusted and reliable Web sites. Also, be sure to **cite** your sources, the same way you would if you were using print materials.

Circle the letter of the best answer to each question below.

1. When you are online, it's safe to give out

   a. your last name.

   b. your first name.

   c. the name of your school.

   d. Both b and c

2. If you use information from a Web site in a school paper, what do you need to do?

   a. Cite your source.

   b. Make sure the information comes from a reliable source.

   c. Ask the Web site for permission.

   d. Both a and b

Read each description below. If you would use informal language in an e-mail to this person, write **IL**. If formal language would be more appropriate, write **FL**.

3. _____ An instant message to your best friend

4. _____ An e-mail thanking your teacher for help with a project

5. _____ A request for information from a NASA scientist

6. _____ An e-mail to your cousin about a party you both attended

Write your answers on the lines below.

7. Why is it risky to download files if you're not sure they come from a trusted source?

   _____

   _____

8. Why isn't it a good idea to share personal information with someone you've met online?

   _____

   _____

9. What do passwords, virus protection programs, and your parents or guardians have in common?

   _____

   _____

alternatives: options or other choices

generate: to create or bring into existence

turbines: rotating engines that work when something, usually a gas or liquid, flows through them

convert: change from one form into another

solar cells: also called *photovoltaic cells*; devices that change light energy into electricity

Wind farms are places where several wind turbines are built in one windy area. Some of the biggest wind farms in California have thousands of wind turbines spinning together to produce energy.

Nearly 20 percent of Denmark's electrical power needs are met by using wind turbines. Germany uses more wind power than any other nation, but it's only six percent of their total electricity needs.

Where can human beings find clean and reliable energy sources?

Human beings meet most of their energy needs by burning fossil fuels. Petroleum is used to make gasoline. Coal is burned to produce electricity. Natural gas is burned to heat our homes. Of course, burning anything creates pollution, but using fossil fuels as an energy source also creates greenhouse gases that affect Earth's atmosphere. Luckily, human beings have other choices. There are **alternatives** to fossil fuels that can be used for energy.

One of the oldest energy sources is also one of the cleanest. Human beings have used wind power for thousands of years. Sailboats captured air currents in their sails and used the energy to move across water. The first windmills were used in Iran more than a thousand years ago. Wind pushed against the blades and made them spin, which then turned gears inside a building. The turning gears were attached to mechanisms that ground corn or pumped water.

Today, wind power is used in a similar way to **generate** electricity. Wind **turbines** are powered by moving air currents. Their giant blades rotate when the wind blows and spin the mechanisms inside the turbine that create electricity. Wind power is quickly becoming a popular alternative to fossil fuels. Since 2000, the amount of electricity created by wind power has increased by more than four times.

Another clean energy source is the sun. Every day, the sun sends more energy down to Earth's surface than human beings could ever use. The problem is that solar energy isn't easy to **convert** into a form useful to human beings. **Solar cells** can change sunlight into electricity, but they are expensive to make compared to the amount of power they produce. As more people use them, though, the price will come down.

Water can also be used to create power. Hydroelectric dams generate electricity by using the falling water to turn giant turbines. After a dam is built, a reservoir builds up behind it, and the weight of the water creates an incredible amount of pressure. Openings in the dam allow this water to flow through, and the pressure turns the turbines and generates electricity. Dams are a clean energy source, but the water in the reservoir could flood the land and disrupt the local ecosystem.

There is no perfect alternative, but as human beings see the consequences of relying too heavily on fossil fuels, these other energy sources will look better and better.

Circle the letter of the best answer to each question below.

1. Which of the following is not a fossil fuel?

    a. coal

    b. natural gas

    c. electricity

    d. petroleum

2. Hydroelectric dams use the _____ of water to turn turbines.

    a. moisture

    b. electromagnetism

    c. fuels

    d. weight

3. The amount of energy the sun sends to Earth each day is _____ the amount of energy human beings need.

    a. much less than

    b. about equal to

    c. much more than

    d. Not enough information is given

Write your answers on the lines below.

4. Choose one of the energy sources from the selection. What is an advantage to using this source that the author didn't already mention?

    _____

5. Now, choose a different energy source from the selection. What is a disadvantage to using this source that the author didn't already mention?

    _____

6. Which energy source from the selection would be best suited for use in a vehicle? Explain your answer.

    _____

    _____

Poisoning the Food Chain

pollutants: substances that contaminate air, water, or soil

concentration: the amount of something in a substance

bioaccumulation: the buildup in the body of chemicals that don't break down or that break down very slowly

biological amplification: the increase in concentrations of chemicals in organisms at higher levels of a food chain

Fish is a high-protein, low-fat food that has a number of health benefits. The omega-3 fatty acids in fish are particularly healthy for the heart. However, the FDA recommends that people limit the amount of fish they eat that are high on the food chain. Consuming large amounts of toxins is dangerous. Mercury can be especially dangerous to unborn babies and to small children.

Why are the biggest fish also the most toxic?

Fish provide food for millions of people all over the world. In coastal communities, people eat fish several times a day. Fish are also important in the balance of nature. They eat plants and animals and, in turn, become food for other living creatures.

The marine food chain begins with tiny floating plants called *phytoplankton* and small animals called *zooplankton*. The next step in the chain is small fish, like bay anchovies, which eat the tiny organisms. Larger fish, like spotted sea trout, eat the smaller fish. Eventually, the sea trout might be caught by a fisherman, who eats the fish or sells it to a store or restaurant. In this food chain, human beings hold a place at the top.

Despite regulations, **pollutants** sometimes make their way from land to the water. Many chemicals are used on farms to kill insects and control weeds. They can perform a useful service to human beings, but they can also be harmful to organisms like fish.

One common toxin found in fish is mercury, a heavy metal on the periodic table. Nature releases mercury in the form of volcanic gases and in the weathering of rocks. Human beings release mercury into the environment by burning waste and using fossil fuels. When pollutants like mercury fall to the ground in the form of rain or snow, they flow into bodies of water. Lakes and streams then carry mercury into the oceans.

The **concentration** of toxins in fish gets stronger and stronger over time because the animals' internal organs can't break down the chemicals. **Bioaccumulation** is the buildup of chemicals that don't break down or that break down very slowly in the body.

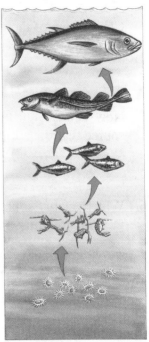

Fish higher up on the food chain survive by eating smaller fish that have been contaminated. They take in more toxins because they eat more. Pollutants can then move up food chains, contaminating the food human beings eat. At each level of the food chain, the concentration of toxins gets higher. This **biological amplification** is the increase in concentrations of chemicals in organisms at higher levels of a food chain.

King mackerel, shark, swordfish, and tilefish contain the highest levels of mercury. However, there are plenty of other fish, such as flounder, sole, wild salmon, and farmed catfish, that are low in mercury and other harmful chemicals. Choose your fish wisely, and it can be a healthful part of your diet.

Circle the letter of the best answer to the question below.

1. _____ are at the bottom of the marine food chain.

   a. Trout

   b. Plankton

   c. Human beings

   d. Anchovies

Write **true** or **false** next to each statement below.

2. _____ Mercury is released into the environment by human beings
   and natural processes.

3. _____ Human beings should stop eating fish because the risks are too high.

4. _____ Pregnant women and young children should not eat fish that contain high
   levels of mercury.

5. _____ Mercury is dangerous to animals but safe for human beings to consume.

Write your answers on the lines below.

6. What does it mean to say that human beings are at the top of the marine food chain?

   _____

7. What are three health benefits to eating fish?

   _____

   _____

8. What is bioaccumulation?

   _____

   _____

9. Explain why the concentration of toxins is higher in large fish than it is in smaller fish.

   _____

   _____

Living in a Wet Land

delta: land located where a river meets a larger body of water; the land is formed by mud and sand that was carried there by the river

climate: the weather conditions in an area

tropics: the area near Earth's equator

monsoon: the heavy rains that occur during a tropical wet season

Bangladesh is one of the most densely populated places on Earth. More than 140 million people, many of whom are farmers, live in an area smaller than Wisconsin.

Trees are chopped down to create fields and to build structures to accommodate the large population. This causes erosion, which makes the flooding even worse.

Why does Bangladesh flood year after year?

The People's Republic of Bangladesh is located in the southeastern part of India. Bangladesh is its own country, but it's almost entirely surrounded by its larger neighbor. In the southern part of Bangladesh, three giant rivers, including the Ganges River, come together and form a **delta**, which is where these rivers flow into the Bay of Bengal in the Indian Ocean.

Bangladesh is about the size of Wisconsin, but its **climate** and landscape couldn't be more different. The land is very flat and very wet. More than 500 different rivers flow through the marshes and jungles that cover the landscape.

Bangladesh is in the **tropics**, so the weather is always hot. There are only three seasons each year—a hot, humid summer, a hot, rainy **monsoon** season, and a hot, dry winter.

The monsoon season is particularly hard on the people of Bangladesh. It lasts from June through September and brings incredible amounts of rain with it. During the summer months, land far from the coasts becomes very hot. During the monsoon season, this warm air rises and pulls moist air from the Indian Ocean onto land. Southern India and Bangladesh get soaked for months with rain as a result. In some areas, more than 12 feet of rain will fall during those wet months.

Bangladesh receives almost all its yearly rainfall during the monsoon season. The land is flat, and it's already wet, so the extra water causes severe flooding. Each year, thousands of people lose their homes. Another problem is that clean sources of drinking water are polluted when water levels rise. Thousands of people get sick each year as well.

Tropical cyclones, also known as *hurricanes*, pose an even greater danger. These powerful storms hit the country every few years and cause incredible amounts of damage. The winds in a cyclone can reach more than 100 miles per hour, and they can bring waves as high as 20 feet crashing into the shore. Because Bangladesh is so flat, these powerful waves rush far inland and flood everything in their path.

Controlling water is an important part of Bangladeshi life. The government of Bangladesh has spent millions of dollars building dams, canals, and other structures to move water away from farms, cities, and homes. In such a wet place, though, this task is difficult and these projects have had only a limited effect.

Circle the letter of the best answer to each question below.

1. Why does Bangladesh flood each year?

    a. The government hasn't built enough dams and canals.

    b. The land can't absorb all the rain that falls during the monsoon season.

    c. Bangladesh is too far from the ocean.

    d. Most of India's water flows into Bangladesh.

2. People get sick during monsoon season because

    a. the clean drinking water gets polluted by the flooding.

    b. the monsoon rains contain bacteria.

    c. the temperatures get much cooler after everything gets wet.

    d. All of the above

Write your answers on the lines below.

3. What causes moist air from the Indian Ocean to move over land during the monsoon season?

    _____

    _____

4. What have human beings done to the land in Bangladesh that has made the flooding worse?

    _____

    _____

Unifying Concepts and Processes

New Orleans, Louisiana, and much of the land surrounding it are part of the Mississippi River Delta. Like Bangladesh, this area is very flat. Use what you learned in this selection to explain why Hurricane Katrina caused so much damage when it hit the area in 2005.

_____

_____

_____

Lesson 6.6   Rising Tide

Does it really matter that the temperatures and sea level on Earth are rising?

Earth is becoming warmer. The change seems gradual, but in terms of Earth's long history, it's happening quickly. In the last 100 years, average temperatures have risen about 1°F. Most scientists believe that this **global warming** is caused in part by human beings' use of fossil fuels, like coal and oil. Burning these materials creates greenhouse gases, like carbon dioxide. The gases act like a blanket in Earth's atmosphere. They trap the heat from the sun, causing the planet to become warmer.

Some effects of global warming are already known. For example, the increase in temperature is causing glaciers and polar ice caps to melt. Warm water also expands, so it takes up more space than cooler water does. This combination has caused sea levels to rise between six and eight inches in the last 100 years.

The problem is that by Earth's standards, this change is coming about too quickly. It doesn't allow ecosystems, animals, or human beings time to adjust. Even a small rise in sea levels—one to two millimeters per year—causes erosion along shores to take place rapidly. One effect is loss of habitat for animals. For example, birds that feed on crabs and crab eggs along the shore have a smaller area to hunt for their meals. You've already learned about the domino effect of changes to one species in the food chain. Remember, nothing in nature happens in **isolation**.

This loss of land is also already changing lives and communities around the world. In low-lying countries, like Bangladesh, people are forced out of their homes every year by rising waters. If the seas rise as scientists predict they will, rice crops will be destroyed there and in other countries. Millions of people will lose their homes and even their villages.

In the U.S., more than half the population lives within 50 miles of a coastline. Higher tides and stronger **storm surges** could completely change the shape of coastal states like Florida within the next century. Even though we can't totally reverse the damage that's been done, human beings have the power to stop the situation from getting worse. Reusing and recycling are good places to start. Walking or riding your bike instead of traveling by car can also make a difference. If everyone does their part, the effects of global warming won't have to be as severe or far-reaching.

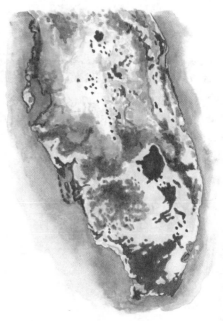

Circle the letter of the best answer to each question below.

1. One reason that sea levels are rising is because

   a. erosion is happening very quickly.

   b. there isn't enough carbon dioxide in Earth's atmosphere.

   c. Earth's warmer temperatures are causing glaciers to melt.

   d. the levels of greenhouse gases have been dropping during the last century.

2. Which of the following is not an effect of rising sea levels?

   a. colder temperatures in the ocean that are dangerous to sea life

   b. increased erosion along shorelines

   c. people losing their homes to high waters

   d. animals losing their natural habitat

Write your answers on the lines below.

3. What do scientists think is a major cause of global warming?

   _____

4. Why is it important to know that the amount of carbon dioxide in the atmosphere is increasing?

   _____

   _____

5. Why did the Cape Hatteras lighthouse have to be moved?

   _____

Unifying Concepts and Processes

Explain what it means to say, "nothing in nature happens in isolation." Then, give an example from another selection you've read to illustrate this point.

   _____

   _____

   _____

   _____

Space travel has been a fact of life since before you were born. Will it always be?

Part of what makes human beings human is their desire to explore the unknown. From the beginning of time, people have pushed their boundaries to see what lay beyond the world they knew. Some of our questions life have been answered, but there is still a lot we don't know.

Advances in technology have made space travel a reality. Ever since human beings landed on the moon in 1969, the possibility of traveling outside of Earth has captured people's imaginations. Many people see the value in space exploration. Others think that the costs are just too high.

No one can argue about the dangers of space travel. Space is not a safe or friendly place for human beings. The conditions are extreme. In order to venture into space, everything needs to be provided for human beings—food, air, water, fuel. They must be protected from cold or hot temperatures, lack of atmosphere, and radiation. Without reliable protection, people would have no chance at all of surviving. This leaves little room for error, either by human beings or by machinery.

Not only is there great risk to human life, but the actual costs of space exploration are enormous. A single space shuttle mission costs about $450 million dollars. Some people think that the money could be better spent on things on Earth, like education and health care.

A good argument can also be made for the benefits of space exploration. Resources on Earth are limited. Alternative sources need to be found, and space is a good place to look. Scientists also want to keep learning about conditions on Mars and the moon. They hope that human beings could one day live somewhere other than Earth.

Technology from the space program has improved life on Earth. For example, materials used in space shuttles have made planes safer and better constructed. A heart pump that was based on a space shuttle fuel pump can help heart patients lead better lives. Exploring space can also help scientists learn more about life on Earth. By collecting data from other planets, they can get a better idea about how our planet formed and how it supports life.

The question of whether or not to continue exploring space isn't an easy one. There are no clear answers. It's a matter of weighing the risks and benefits. What's your opinion?

In late 2006, NASA announced its plans to build a base on the moon. By the year 2024, a rotating crew of people will live there, which will be similar to the way the International Space Station operates today.

When the space shuttle *Challenger* exploded after launch in 1986, seven astronauts died. In 2003, seven more astronauts lost their lives when the space shuttle *Columbia* broke up on re-entry into Earth's atmosphere. These events made many people question whether it was too risky to send human beings into space.

Space exploration doesn't have to be all or nothing. It is much less risky and expensive to send robots into space instead of human beings. They can collect data and perform some experiments. They don't have all the abilities a human astronaut does, but some people believe that robot-manned missions are a good compromise.

Circle the letter of the best answer to the question below.

1. Space travel is dangerous for human beings because

   a. the conditions in space are similar to conditions on Earth.

   b. it is very expensive.

   c. they can't survive without a lot of equipment.

   d. technology hasn't advanced very much in recent years.

Write **true** or **false** next to each statement below.

2. _____ Human beings are curious about the unknown.

3. _____ NASA has been operating a base on the moon for more than 20 years.

4. _____ Scientists hope to find resources in space that could be useful to human beings.

5. _____ Not everyone agrees about the value and importance of space exploration.

6. _____ Technology developed for the space program has no use on Earth.

Write your answers on the lines below.

7. How did the two space shuttle disasters affect the public's view of space travel?

   _____

   _____

8. What is one benefit and one drawback of using robots instead of human beings for space exploration?

   _____

   _____

9. Why do some people think that the use of money for space exploration is a bad decision?

   _____

   _____

10. What do you think about space exploration? Are the risks worth the benefits? Explain.

    _____

    _____

Circle the letter of the best answer to each question below.

1. Which of the following is not good online behavior?

   a. You send an informal e-mail to a friend on your soccer team.

   b. You look up information about horses at the Web site of an online encyclopedia.

   c. You download a popular song from a Web site you've never visited before.

   d. You use a photo you found online to illustrate a report and include your source.

2. Rising sea levels will

   a. have little effect on human populations.

   b. flood low, flat coastal areas.

   c. destroy the homes and neighborhoods of many people that live in coastal areas.

   d. Both b and c

Write **true** or **false** next to each statement below.

3. _____ People didn't bathe during the Renaissance because they thought water would make them sick.

4. _____ As long as you always pay to download songs or videos, you can be sure your computer won't pick up a virus.

5. _____ The amount of energy the sun sends to Earth each day is many times the amount human beings use.

6. _____ All the mercury that pollutes the oceans was created by human beings.

7. _____ Hurricanes are also called *tropical cyclones*.

8. _____ Technology from the space program has many uses on Earth, too.

9. _____ As long as average temperatures rise only a few degrees, the effects on the environment won't be noticeable.

Write your answers on the lines below.

10. What is personal hygiene, and why is it important?

   _____

   _____

11. Explain how bathing in Greek and Roman times was different than it is today.

_____

12. When is it okay to give out more than your first name online?

_____

13. Why is wind power a good alternative to fossil fuels?

_____

14. Solar cells have been around for many years now, but they still aren't widely used as a source of electrical energy. Why not?

_____

15. Why do fish high in the food chain contain the most toxins?

_____

16. What are the risks and benefits of eating fish?

_____

_____

17. Describe what the monsoon season is like in Bangladesh.

_____

18. Give two reasons why tropical cyclones cause so much damage to the coastal areas of Bangladesh.

_____

19. How are human beings contributing to global warming?

_____

20. What are two arguments in favor of space exploration?

_____

_____

21. What two major events caused many people to question the need for space exploration?

_____

Lesson 7.1 An Atomic Time Line

philosophers: people who study the nature and meaning of life

Dark Ages: a period in European history that lasted from A.D. 476 to about A.D. 1000, in which work in the arts and sciences was discouraged

Law of Conservation of Mass: Lavoisier's theory that matter is never created or destroyed, it just changes form

chemical compounds: substances that contain the atoms of two or more elements that have combined to form molecules; water is a chemical compound that contains molecules made of hydrogen and oxygen atoms

This timeline contains the work of a lot of different men, but women have also been a part of atomic history. Madame Lavoisier worked alongside her husband Antoine in their laboratory. Marie Curie studied radioactive materials and is the only woman to win two Nobel Prizes. Lise Meitner helped discover nuclear fission.

How did human beings discover that all matter is made of atoms?

450 B.C.—The Greek **philosophers** Democritus and Leucippus suggested that all matter is made of tiny particles called *atomos*, a Greek word meaning *uncuttable*.

A.D. 1100—While Europe was experiencing the **Dark Ages**, the idea of atoms was kept alive in the Islamic Empire by scholars like al-Ghazali.

1789—Antoine Lavoisier showed that elements are substances that can't be broken down into any simpler substances. He also described the **Law of Conservation of Mass**.

1803—What we know about atoms today really begins with John Dalton. He used Lavoiser's discoveries to show that the reason elements can't be created or destroyed is because they are made of "uncuttable" particles, or atoms. Dalton also proved that each element is made of its own kind of atom, and that these atoms combine in different ways to form **chemical compounds**.

1827—A botanist named Robert Brown used a microscope to observe pollen particles floating in water. The tiny pieces never stopped moving, so Brown wondered if they might be alive. He sprinkled dust, which he knew wasn't alive, into the water instead and saw the same constant motion. Why were the particles moving? The theory became known as "Brownian motion."

1897—J. J. Thomson's experiments with electricity and gas showed that atoms contain even smaller particles with negative electrical charges. He called the particles *corpuscles*, but they're better known today as *electrons*.

1905—Albert Einstein wrote a paper about Brownian motion. He used math to prove that Brown's pollen particles kept moving because the water was made of tiny molecules in motion. This paper became the first solid proof that atoms and molecules exist.

1909—Hans Geiger and Ernest Marsden shot tiny particles through a sheet of gold. Most of the particles sailed right through, but once in a while a particle bounced away. Ernest Rutherford used this experiment to show that atoms are mostly filled with empty space. At the center of each atom is a solid nucleus—that's what a few of the particles bumped into. Electrons buzz around the nucleus, but between the nucleus and electrons is a lot of space. That's why most of the particles could fly right through the sheet of gold. Rutherford had discovered the structure of the atom.

Circle the letter of the best answer to each question below.

1. The idea that matter is made up of tiny particles has been around since at least

   a. the time of the ancient Greeks.

   b. Albert Einstein suggested the idea.

   c. the Islamic Empire.

   d. Lavoisier proved the existence of atoms.

2. Particles could sail right through the sheet of gold because

   a. gold has tiny atoms.

   b. atoms are mostly filled with empty space.

   c. gold doesn't contain many atoms.

   d. they were moving very quickly.

Number the following events in the order in which they occurred.

3. _____ Einstein used math to prove the existence of atoms and molecules.

4. _____ Brown observed particles of pollen moving in water.

5. _____ Rutherford explained the structures of atoms.

6. _____ J. J. Thomson discovered electrons.

7. _____ Geiger and Marsden shot tiny particles through a sheet of gold.

Write your answers on the lines below.

8. What caused "Brownian motion"?

   _____

9. What did Einstein's and Dalton's discoveries have in common?

   _____

Unifying Concepts and Processes

Why do you think the discovery of atoms took such a long time and involved so many people?

_____

_____

The Golden Age of Islamic Science

economy: the way money and goods are distributed

refraction: how rays of light bend when they move from one medium into another

Persian: a person from Persia, an area of the Middle East that is known as Iran today

diagnosis: identification of a disease by looking at symptoms

Alhazen invented the first *camera obscura*, which is a box with a small hole in one side. Inside the dark box, light enters through the hole and projects an image onto the opposite side. The cameras we use today developed from this idea.

Alhazen was also an astronomer. A crater on the moon was named in his honor.

What other scientific contributions have Islamic scholars made?

For nearly 600 years—from A.D. 650 to about A.D. 1250—an Islamic empire ruled much of the world. Its lands stretched from Spain in the west, across North Africa and the Middle East, to the edges of China and India. Trade was an important part of the empire's **economy**, so citizens traveled often to the major cities to sell their products.

Millions of people gathered each year in the city of Mecca as well. In the religion of Islam, each Muslim tries to visit Mecca at least once in his or her lifetime. People who traveled to Mecca and the other big cities brought ideas about art, literature, and science with them. These places became thriving centers for learning and discovery.

In A.D. 830, Mūsā al-Khwārizmī, an Islamic scholar, wrote a book that changed mathematics forever. He showed that calculations could be made using symbols in place of some numbers. Geometry and most advanced forms of math use al-Khwārizmī's system, better known today as *algebra*.

One of Islam's greatest scientists was Alhazen. His *Book of Optics* argued correctly that we see when rays of light enter the eye. Until then, most people thought that rays came out of our eyes to help us see. Alhazen also made discoveries about **refraction** and the colors in white light. He used this knowledge to write about rainbows and why the sky changes colors during sunsets.

Alhazen's greatest contribution, though, might be his use of experiments. Alhazen and other Islamic scientists showed that a hypothesis could be tested with a well-designed experiment. They were the first scientists to use the scientific method.

Avicenna was a **Persian** doctor and scientist. His most famous book was the *Canon of Medicine*. It described diseases, drugs, treatments, and cures. Avicenna knew that it was important to prevent illness and realized that a careful **diagnosis** needed to be made so that the correct treatment could be provided. For more than 500 years, Avicenna's *Canon* was the medical reference used by doctors throughout Europe.

While Europe experienced the Dark Ages, the Islamic Empire continued the tradition of scientific inquiry begun by the Greeks and Romans. When the Renaissance finally swept through Europe, it was fueled partly by knowledge learned from the scholars of Islam.

Circle the letter of the best answer to each question below.

1. What is algebra?

   a. a type of math that uses symbols

   b. a type of telescope invented by Alhazen

   c. a medicine named after an Islamic scholar

   d. a big city located in the Islamic Empire

2. Many Islamic scientists used _____ to make their scientific discoveries.

   a. diagnosis

   b. refraction

   c. experiments

   d. symbols

Write your answers on the lines below.

3. How did Alhazen's *Book of Optics* change the way people understood vision?

   _____

   _____

4. Why did the big cities of the Islamic Empire become important centers of learning?

   _____

   _____

5. One of the steps in the scientific method is to share the results of an experiment or discovery. How does the selection show this part of the scientific method in action?

   _____

   _____

6. Today, scientists make new medical discoveries all the time. New articles are published each year that contain the latest information. For nearly 500 years, though, Avicenna's *Canon of Medicine* was the best medical textbook available. Why do you think it was used for such a long time?

   _____

   _____

Industrial Revolution: the period lasting from about 1760 to 1850, in which engines, machines, and factories became the main way that things were made

manual labor: physical work that is done by hand

mechanized: used machines in place of work that was done by hand

Before the Industrial Revolution, books were considered a luxury for the wealthy. Many people couldn't read or write. It was common for them to sign important documents with an X instead of their names. After the printing industry began using steam power, though, reading material became affordable to almost everyone. Paper was cheap, so newspapers and popular books were sold in many places. This change encouraged more people to learn to read. It also meant that more people began paying attention to politics, the government, and the economy.

How do inventions from the 1700s still affect our lives today?

Before the **Industrial Revolution**, the production of most goods was limited by the amount of **manual labor** each worker could handle. It cost a lot of money to pay another person to make something, so people made many things themselves, especially clothing.

When steam engines were invented in the late 1700s, they changed how most goods were made. A steam engine uses pressure from trapped steam as an energy source. Machines had been around for a while, but they were powered by water flowing in streams and rivers. The weight of moving water turned a giant waterwheel, and then this kinetic energy was used to saw lumber or grind grain. These machines could only be built along waterways, though. Steam engines could be built anywhere, and engineers found many different uses for them.

During this same time, improvements were also made in metal tools. Gears, pistons, and other machine parts became stronger and easier to manufacture. Bigger and faster machines were built, and steam power was available to run them. A new kind of building was needed to hold these machines and the people who ran them. These buildings were factories. The Industrial Revolution was underway.

Suddenly, one worker could accomplish more in a day using a machine than had ever been possible before. Labor costs fell, so the amount people paid for these goods fell, too. Demand increased for the new, inexpensive products, so more factories were built and more workers were hired.

Thousands of people moved to the cities to work in factories. Cities became overcrowded and unsafe. Each new factory also meant another smokestack. Soon, the skies of many big cities darkened with pollution.

The changes caused by the Industrial Revolution provided many different opportunities. Railroads and steamships could ship products quickly around the world. The growing populations meant that cities needed new roads and sewer systems. There was also a demand for other professions, like doctors, teachers, police officers, and firefighters.

Over time, many of the Industrial Revolution's worst problems were addressed. Today, we know that the **mechanized** production of goods can have benefits for everyone.

Circle the letter of the best answer to the question below.

1. The Industrial Revolution occurred

   a. about 100 years ago.

   b. about 200 years ago.

   c. about 500 years ago.

   d. about 1000 years ago.

Write your answers on the lines below.

2. Machines work more quickly than human beings do. What is another benefit to using a machine instead of manual labor?

   _____

   _____

3. How did the use of steam engines change the way machines could be used?

   _____

   _____

4. Describe one positive change and one negative change brought about by the Industrial Revolution.

   _____

   _____

5. Steam is water in the form of a gas, so it isn't pollution. If steam engines were being used for power in the factories of the Industrial Revolution, what do you think was causing all of the pollution? [Hint: How is liquid water turned into steam?]

   _____

   _____

6. What effect did technology have on rates of literacy, or people's ability to read? Why?

   _____

   _____

The Need for Speed

internal combustion engine: an engine that is powered by the energy of explosions; the explosions occur when mixtures of gasoline and air are ignited

rocket engine: an internal combustion engine that is open at one end; as the exploding fuel pushes out of the opening, the vehicle is pushed in the opposite direction

speed of sound: at sea level, sound waves move at about 770 miles per hour; higher in Earth's atmosphere, they travel more slowly

Soon after Verne's story was published, a woman named Nellie Bly set out to see how quickly she could circle the globe. In 1889, Bly managed to make it around the world in 72 days traveling alone.

What's the fastest speed you've ever traveled?

In 1873, Jules Verne published his adventure story *Around the World in Eighty Days*. At the time, circling the globe in 80 days seemed nearly impossible, so it was an exciting idea. Verne knew his novel's plot wasn't complete science fiction, though. The Industrial Revolution had changed the world. Railroads stretched across America and much of Asia. Steam-powered ships carried people across the oceans in record time.

Getting from place to place as quickly as possible became more important to human beings. With each advance in technology, the top speed that human beings could travel increased as well.

Long ago, human beings got around only by foot. A runner might reach 20 miles per hour for a short distance, but walkers moved at less than five miles per hour. Around 2000 B.C., human beings began using horses. Horses can travel farther without getting as tired, and a galloping horse can race along at 40 miles per hour. Just like human beings, though, horses need to rest, drink, and eat.

The swift current of a stream or river was another way people and goods moved quickly across long distances. At sea, sails captured the wind and moved ships across the water. Of course, waterways could carry people only to places near water. This is why many of the world's oldest and biggest cities are located on rivers and along coasts.

The invention of steam engines brought a major change to the way human beings moved around. A train rolling along smooth tracks could cover huge distances in little time. The first travelers to head across America spent months making the journey. The same trip by train took only a few days. Steamships made ocean journeys much faster as well. They cut the time it took to cross the Atlantic Ocean from about one month using sails, to a couple of weeks using steam.

During the 20th century, the **internal combustion engine** made travel even faster. As engines continued to get better, they got faster. By 1927, racecars were speeding along the ground at more than 200 miles per hour.

One of the most important milestones in the history of speed occurred on October 14, 1947. Pilot Chuck Yeager flew an experimental airplane that used a **rocket engine**. He became the first human being to travel faster than the **speed of sound**, hurtling along at nearly 700 miles per hour.

Circle the letter of the best answer to each question below.

1. How fast do human beings walk?

   a. about 3 or 4 miles per hour

   b. about 20 miles per hour

   c. less than 1 mile per hour

   d. about 1 mile per day

2. Chuck Yeager was the first human being

   a. to travel around the world.

   b. to fly faster than the speed of light.

   c. to fly faster than the speed of sound.

   d. to race a car faster than 200 miles per hour.

Write your answers on the lines below.

3. Why are so many of the world's oldest and biggest cities located near bodies of water?

   _____

   _____

4. The first automobiles didn't get people around any faster than horses could, but cars still steadily replaced the use of animals for transportation. Give at least two reasons why you think this happened.

   _____

   _____

5. Space shuttles zoom astronauts around Earth at the incredible speed of 17,000 miles per hour. No vehicle moving on land or in Earth's atmosphere can even come close to that speed. Why do you think vehicles can move so much more quickly in space?

   _____

   _____

What's Next?

For as long as cars have been around, people have been racing them to see how fast they can go. What is the fastest speed anyone has ever reached on land? What kind of vehicle did they use? Has anyone ever traveled faster than the speed of sound in a car? Do some research to find the answers.

Carving Out a Place in History

depletes: uses up; reduces in amount

crop rotation: the process of growing different crops in the same place to avoid stripping the soil of nutrients

legume: a family of protein-rich food plants that includes peas, beans, and peanuts

nitrogen: an element that makes up 78% of the atmosphere and is found in all living tissues

"He could have added fortune to fame, but caring for neither, he found happiness and honor in being helpful to the world."
—quote on George Washington Carver's grave

Carver is best remembered for his work as a scientist, but he was also an accomplished artist, singer, poet, and pianist.

Few of Carver's peanut, soybean, and sweet potato inventions were ever turned into widely-used products. He kept the formulas in his head and didn't write many down, so others weren't able to create the products he developed.

How did one man change the lives of hundreds of farmers?

In many ways, George Washington Carver is a classic example of an American success story. Carver was born into slavery in Missouri around the time of the Civil War. He lost his mother at an early age and stayed on the farm where he was born for several years after slavery was abolished. Because illness had made him weak, physical labor was difficult for him. As a result, Carver spent time outdoors, observing plants and animals and developing a lifelong interest in the natural world.

Carver slowly worked his way through school. He was accepted at one college but then later rejected when they found out he was African American. He tried again and eventually received both his bachelor's and master's degrees in science.

Carver spent his career at Alabama's Tuskegee Institute teaching and doing agricultural research. These two areas—research and education—are where Carver really left his mark. For years, the South had depended almost completely on cotton crops. This had left the land in bad shape. Growing only a single type of crop **depletes** the soil of nutrients. Carver understood the importance of **crop rotation** and encouraged farmers to changed their crops from year to year. He was determined to share his knowledge and help poor southern farmers, many of whom were African American.

Carver urged farmers to plant crops from the **legume** family, such as peanuts and soybeans. These crops had two major benefits—they provided a good source of protein for southerners, and they would restore **nitrogen** to the soil. Nitrogen is an important element in keeping soil healthy so that it can nourish crops. Carver also encouraged farmers to plant sweet potatoes. Many took his advice but found they had difficulty selling the products of these crops. Carver solved this problem by putting together a series of bulletins. They explained dozens of ways peanuts and sweet potatoes could be used in many products, including flour, coffee, soap, and dyes.

When an insect called the *boll weevil* destroyed cotton plants in the early 1900s, more and more farmers turned to Carver's ideas for alternative crops. Peanuts had not even been recognized as a crop around the turn of the century. By 1940, they were the second largest cash crop in the South. Farmers were no longer dependent on only one crop for their success or failure. George Washington Carver had succeeded in improving the quality of life for poor southern farmers.

Circle the letter of the best answer to each question below.

1. George Washington Carver is best known for his research with

   a. nitrogen.

   b. peanuts and sweet potatoes.

   c. cotton.

   d. pesticides.

2. What is one effect of growing only a single type of crop?

   a. Only that type of crop will be able to grow in the soil.

   b. Farmers have to depend on the success of just one crop.

   c. The soil is depleted of certain types of nutrients.

   d. Both b and c

Write your answers on the lines below.

3. What problem did farmers have once they started planting the crops that Carver recommended?

   _____

4. How did Carver address this problem?

   _____

5. Carver didn't write down the formulas for many of the products he invented. How does this set him apart from most other scientists?

   _____

6. If others adopted similar habits, how might the world of science change?

   _____

Use the words in the box to complete the sentences below.

alternative	agriculture	boll weevils

7. _____ were a threat to cotton crops.

8. Carver hoped that farmers would plant _____ crops.

9. Although Carver had many talents, _____ was his specialty.

Spreading the Word

pesticides: substances, often poisonous, which are used to kill pests

banning: stopping the use of something

"We do not inherit the earth from our ancestors, we borrow it from our children."
—Native American proverb

In spite of its dangers, DDT has been a useful pesticide. Malaria is a disease spread by mosquitoes. More than 75 million cases were reported in India before the use of DDT. After using it for 10 years, the number of cases shrank to about 5 million. One major problem, though, was that insects were becoming resistant to DDT. The pesticide also often killed their predators, leaving larger, stronger populations of the harmful insect.

DDT is no longer used to protect crops in most countries. It is still sometimes used, though, to combat diseases that are spread by insects.

Do pesticides kill more than just insects?

Rachel Carson had two main loves in her life—writing and the natural world. She had spent much time exploring the plant and animal life around her childhood home with her mother. She was a talented writer, too, and decided to major in English and creative writing in college. When she was halfway through her studies, she decided to change her major to zoology. She had no idea at the time how famous she would become by combining her two talents.

Carson continued her schooling and worked for years as a marine biologist. She had a great love and respect for the seas and the creatures that lived there. She wrote three books about the oceans and shared with others her beliefs about the importance of preserving them.

In the 1940s, Carson began learning about the use of **pesticides** in the United States. She was very concerned about the way that new pesticides, especially one called *DDT*, were being used. She researched the topic and the more she learned, the more she felt the need to make other Americans aware of what was happening. She wanted people to understand that all life is connected. Even though a pesticide might target a limited number of insects, the effects reached much further than that. Not only could other animals on the food chain feel the effects of the poisons, so could human beings.

Carson began writing a book she titled *Silent Spring*. The title referred to what Carson predicted might happen if the way pesticides were used didn't change: there would be so few birds left that there would be silence in the air instead of birdsong in the spring. Even before the book was published in 1962, there was a strong reaction against it and its author. Chemical companies attacked Carson, saying that the book wasn't based on science and that she was only a hysterical woman. There were even threats of lawsuits. Carson did her best not to pay attention. She was confident that she had an important message to share.

Readers saw the sense in what Carson had to say, and *Silent Spring* became a huge bestseller. Readers saw the sense in what Carson had to say. The book kicked off the environmental movement. It also made the heavy use of pesticides a public issue.

Rachel Carson died in 1964 at the age of 56. She did not live long enough to see the **banning** of DDT in 1972. Even so, she knew she had made a difference in the world and that others would pick up the fight.

Write **true** or **false** next to each statement below.

1. _____ After *Silent Spring* was published, DDT was found to be safe for human beings.

2. _____ Rachel Carson was a well-known marine biologist.

3. _____ Over time, some insects can become resistant to DDT.

4. _____ Carson named her book *Silent Spring* because she predicted that pesticides would pollute all the water in natural springs.

5. _____ The use of DDT can stop the spread of some diseases by insects.

Write your answers on the lines below.

6. Why were Carson's writing skills important to her as a scientist?

   _____

7. Why did the release of *Silent Spring* make chemical companies so angry?

   _____

8. What place does *Silent Spring* have in the history of environmental action?

   _____

9. Even though DDT is a toxic chemical, using it in certain situations is still allowed. Do you think the benefits outweigh the risks in these cases?

   _____

   _____

Unifying Concepts and Processes

1. What do you think critics of genetically modified foods might have had in common with Rachel Carson?

   _____

   _____

2. In the selection about toxic fish, you learned about biological amplification. Do you think the same concept could be applied to the use of pesticides? Explain.

   _____

Playing with Your Television

programs:
instructions that tell a
computer what to do

monitor: a screen
used for displaying
images or information

graphics: images
created by a computer
and displayed on a
screen or printer

hardware: the
physical equipment
used by a computer

software: the
nonphysical programs
that run a computer

Video game arcades
today specialize in
games that people
don't have at home.
Big machines with
dance floors,
motorcycles, racecars,
and sports equipment
fill the arcades of the
21st century.

Today, people don't
even have to be in the
same room in order to
play a video game
with each other. The
Internet allows them
to be anywhere in the
world while they
compete.

MMOGs, or
massively multiplayer
online games, are
Internet games that
thousands of people
can participate in at
the same time.

When did people first begin playing video games?

People love playing games, so it's no surprise that almost as soon as computers were invented, someone found a way to use them for games. The first modern computers were developed in the 1940s. By the early 1950s, simple checkers and tic-tac-toe **programs** had been written for them. Only the programmers played these first computer games, though. It would still be a few years before video games were introduced to the public.

In 1972, the first home video game system was developed. It had a console that plugged into any TV and several game cartridges that plugged into the console. Playing games on a TV was a brand-new idea, and many people thought they needed a special TV in order for the equipment to work. These first video game systems didn't sell well.

Then, a year later, came Pong. This game was a simple version of tennis that two people could play at once. Pong was a huge hit in arcades across America, and the game became a big fad. In 1975, a home version of the game was developed that plugged into a television. People lined up outside of stores to buy the game. No one doubted the popularity of home video game systems any longer.

After Pong, a video game craze swept the country. From the late 1970s through the mid 1980s, arcades sprang up across the country. At the same time, home video game systems continued to improve. By the end of the 80s, most video and computer games were being played at home. Arcades began going out of business.

Video games differ from other electronic games, like pinball or air hockey, because the action takes place on a **monitor**. Early video games had very simple **graphics**. Images on the screen were made with dots, lines, and bars. Most of the screen was filled with empty space.

During the 1990s, **hardware** used in computers and video games got much smaller and faster, so the **software** could contain more and more information. Video game graphics, sounds, and movements became more complex and realistic.

Today, video games are still played on computer monitors and TVs, but they can also be played on tiny cell phones and MP3 players. Video games may have begun as a fad, but they're now a common part of the entertainment world, alongside movies, television, and music.

Circle the letter of the best answer to each question below.

1. All video games
   a. are played in arcades.
   b. are played on monitors.
   c. are played on computers.
   d. are played at home.

2. All video games
   a. use hardware.
   b. use software.
   c. use video game cartridges.
   d. Both a and b

Write your answers on the lines below.

3. Describe how video game graphics are different now compared to when video games were first developed.

   _____

4. How is the history of video games related to the history of computers?

   _____

5. What happened in computer technology that allowed video games to be played on cell phones?

   _____

6. Why do you think video game technology improved only after Pong and other video games became extremely popular?

   _____

   _____

What's Next?

The amount of information used by a video game was measured in bits. For example, a 64-bit game is faster and more complex than a 32-bit game. Computer memory is measured in bytes. Do some research find out what a bit is and how it's different from a byte.

Circle the letter of the best answer to each question below.

1. Einstein used _____ to prove that atoms and molecules exist.

   a. sheets of gold

   b. Brownian motion

   c. neutrons and protons

   d. oxygen and hydrogen

2. Which of the following statements is not true?

   a. Astronauts commonly orbit Earth at 17,000 miles per hour.

   b. Steamships could cross the Atlantic Ocean in just a couple of weeks.

   c. Some spacecraft can travel faster than the speed of light.

   d. The first cars weren't any faster than horses.

3. Today, the pesticide DDT

   a. is no longer used at all because of the book *Silent Spring*.

   b. is still used to treat certain diseases.

   c. is only used to kill insects that damage important crops.

   d. is used sometimes to help stop the spread of disease.

4. Video games were first sold to the public during the

   a. 1990s.

   b. 1980s.

   c. 1970s.

   d. 1950s.

Write your answers on the lines below.

5. Which atomic particles were discovered first: electrons, protons, or neutrons? _____

6. The _____ was first used by Islamic scientists to prove or disprove hypotheses.

7. Give one example of a discovery or invention made by an Islamic scientist.

   _____

8. Explain how steam engines made the Industrial Revolution possible.

_____

9. Name at least two changes that occurred in society as a result of the Industrial Revolution.

_____

10. Why was water the best way to travel before engines were invented?

_____

11. What important advice did George Washington Carver give to farmers in the South?

_____

12. Carver found dozens of uses for _____ and _____, two common southern crops today.

13. Why didn't many of Carver's discoveries become widely used?

_____

14. Why did Rachel Carson title her book *Silent Spring*?

_____

15. What affect did the publication of *Silent Spring* have on society?

_____

16. Name two things that video games and computers have in common.

_____

Draw a line from the word or phrase in column one to its definition in column two.

17. chemical compound   **a.** identification of a disease by looking at symptoms

18. hardware   **b.** use machines in place of work that was done by hand

19. diagnosis   **c.** uses up or reduces in amount

20. programs   **d.** a substance containing molecules

21. legume   **e.** protein-rich food plant

22. mechanize   **f.** the physical equipment used by a computer

23. depletes   **g.** instructions that tell a computer what to do

Final Test

Circle the letter of the best answer to each question below.

1. An atom with a negative electrical charge

   a. has more electrons than protons.

   b. has more protons than electrons.

   c. has no neutrons.

   d. has equal numbers of protons and electrons.

2. Which of the following is not an adaptation of desert plants?

   a. becoming dormant

   b. having very long roots

   c. having few leaves

   d. having thin, brittle leaves

3. A laser beam contains

   a. several different wavelengths of light.

   b. one wavelength of light.

   c. white light in a concentrated form.

   d. microwaves.

4. The invention of the steam engine

   a. helped bring about the Industrial Revolution.

   b. decreased the amount of time it took to get from place to place.

   c. replaced the internal combustion engine.

   d. Both a and b

5. Pong was one of the most important video games because

   a. it was the first game to use a computer.

   b. it was the first game that sold well.

   c. it was the first electronic game.

   d. it was the first game that used a video monitor.

Underline the correct answer from the two choices you are given.

6. Scientists gather (data, conclusions) to prove or disprove hypotheses.

7. Two (dominant, recessive) genes will produce the trait of the recessive gene.

8. Positive charges (repel, attract) other positive charges.

9. A person skiing down a mountain is an example of (potential, kinetic) energy.

10. Sound moves faster through (solids, gases) than through liquids.

11. *Echolocation* is the use of (hertz, vibrations) to locate objects.

12. The (autonomic, peripheral) nervous system controls involuntary activities.

13. Wind is caused by differences in (chemicals, temperature) in Earth's atmosphere.

Write your answers on the lines below.

14. What is erosion?

   _____

15. List two of the three scales used to measure thermal energy.

   _____   _____

16. What did the invention of the airplane and the discovery of the atom have in common?

   _____

17. List two safety measures that are important to remember when working in a lab.

   _____

18. Give two examples of electromagnetic radiation. _____   _____

19. What makes elements different from other substances?

   _____

20. What kind of relationship do the plants and animals of a biome have with one another?

   _____

21. Why did the wolves disappear in the West, and why have they been reintroduced?

   _____

   _____

22. Explain what it means for two species to coevolve.

_____

23. When you learn something new, you are creating pathways between _____.

24. What does *nature versus nurture* mean?

_____

25. Describe two things scientists know about Earth's crust.

_____

26. What human activity produces greenhouse gases?

_____

27. Explain the role of plants in the oxygen cycle.

_____

28. Name two types of objects other than planets that orbit the sun.

_____   _____

29. What characteristic did Hubble use to classify galaxies? _____

30. Our solar system is part of the _____ galaxy.

31. What does a seismograph measure? _____

32. How were both the printing press and Islamic scientists a part of the Renaissance?

_____

33. What safety measures can you take to protect your computer from viruses?

_____

34. How is a digital camera different from a traditional camera?

_____

35. What are the two main reasons roads need to be repaved often?

_____   _____

36. Choose an alternative to fossil fuels and give one benefit and one drawback to using it.

_____

37. Explain what role the food chain has in fish toxicity.

_____

38. Number the following events in order of when they occurred.

_____ Dinosaurs became extinct.

_____ Bacteria and other simple life forms appeared.

_____ The first human beings evolved.

_____ Bubbling lava and steam covered Earth's surface.

_____ The Cambrian Explosion took place.

Write **true** or **false** next to each statement below.

39. _____ Ocean waves are a form of mechanical weathering.

40. _____ Absolute zero exists only in theory and has never actually been reached.

41. _____ Electricity is the movement of protons from one atom to another.

42. _____ The relationship between a pollinator and a flower is called mutualism.

43. _____ Today, Pluto is considered an asteroid, not a planet.

44. _____ The invention of GM foods created an alternative to selective breeding.

45. _____ The main purpose of artificial satellites is to gather and share information.

Draw a line to match each scientist with his or her discovery or invention.

46. Gregor Mendel   **a.** invented the camera obscura

47. George Washington Carver   **b.** discovered dominant and recessive traits

48. Copernicus   **c.** designed the periodic table

49. Alhazen   **d.** developed the idea that Earth revolves around the sun

50. Rachel Carson   **e.** promoted crop rotation

51. Dmitri Mendeleyev   **f.** told people about the dangers of pesticides

Page 7

1. Day 7
2. Day 16
3. Day 7
4. Days 2 and 11
5. 2.5 inches
6. false
7. false
8. true
9. true
10. Possible answer: No. This chart only tracks the weather as it was for three specific weeks. The weather during another month will be different.
11. Possible answer: Yes. The data the students collected showed that each time it rained, the barometric pressure did drop in the days before the rain came.

Page 9

1. d
2. a
3. red
4. red; yellow; red
5. Possible answer: He wanted to make sure that he controlled which plants bred with one another so that he could track the results.
6. Possible answer: He wasn't a professional scientist.
7. Possible answer: They probably would have gotten the same results.

Page 11

1. d
2. a
3. Possible answer: Weathering is the breaking down of rock, while erosion is the movement of rock that has already been broken down.
4. Possible answer: When water freezes it expands. If it keeps freezing and then thawing, this can create pressure that causes the rock to crack or break apart.
5. Possible answer: Human beings have removed trees, which causes land to erode more quickly.
6. Possible answer: Hurricanes and tornadoes have high winds and heavy rains. Wind and rain are both agents of erosion.
7. Glaciers can break down rock (weathering) and move it (erosion).

Page 13

1. a
2. d
3. d
4. Water freezes at 0°C and boils at 100°C.
5. Possible answer: Degrees in the Kelvin scale are equal to degrees Celsius. The Kelvin scale starts at absolute zero. The Celsius scale starts at the temperature at which water freezes.

6. Possible answer: Absolute zero is the temperature at which molecules stop moving and there is no thermal energy.

7. 14.56°C

Page 15

1. b

2. a

3. Possible answer: The beaches were soft and flat, and there was a strong, steady wind.

4. Possible answer: No. Others had been working on flying machines before them, so they used some of their ideas and mechanisms.

5. Possible answer: Yes. They didn't give up until they had found a solution, and they learned from what other inventors had discovered.

Unifying Concepts and Processes

Possible answer: Many different people contributed to the invention of the automobile. Testing airplanes was more dangerous than testing cars.

Page 17

1. Possible answers: Erika's shirt is baggy, her jewelry is dangly, and she's wearing sandals. She's also eating in the lab, and her hair is not tied back.

2. true

3. false

4. false

5. true

6. safety glasses; apron; gloves

7. so you know exactly what you are supposed to do and you are aware of any possible dangers

8. Possible answers: She should read the instructions carefully. She should wear gloves, safety glasses, and an apron.

Page 19

1. habitable

2. atmosphere

3. Technology

4. Exoplanets

5. Possible answer: Creativity helps scientists think of good questions to ask. It helps them explore the natural world and come up with original ideas.

6. They are all signs that a planet might be able to support life.

7. Possible answer: Study a range of maths and sciences, and try to get a firsthand look at what it is actually like to be a scientist.

8. Because there are billions of stars and billions of galaxies, it seems likely that other planets have Earth-like conditions.

9. Possible answer: A computer allows Seager to create models of exoplanet atmospheres, even though she doesn't know exactly what those atmospheres are like. It lets her test different combinations and possibilities.

Unifying Concepts and Processes

Possible answer: By making predictions, scientists can come up with hypotheses to test. A prediction doesn't have to be correct to be valuable, because it can let a scientist know if he or she is on the right track.

Page 20

1. d
2. b
3. d
4. a
5. so his or her research is reliable and nothing gets forgotten
6. No one paid attention to his research or took him seriously because he wasn't a trained scientist.

Page 21

7. Weathering needs to occur before erosion can take place. Weathering breaks down rock into small pieces that can be moved by wind or water.
8. water
9. Absolute zero is reached when molecules and atoms stop moving because there is no thermal energy. In reality, molecules and atoms never stop moving completely.
10. Possible answer: The Wright Brothers knew that they needed to focus on the problem of controlling the flying machine.
11. Possible answers: You shouldn't wear sandals, you shouldn't eat or drink in the lab, and you should check with an adult before starting an experiment.
12. Possible answers: The planet might be habitable. It might be able to support life.
13. contaminated
14. energy
15. conclusions
16. Genes
17. practical
18. analyze

Page 23

1. b
2. a
3. a
4. The nucleus is the center of the atom, where protons and neutrons are found.
5. Possible answer: Electrons move from atoms with negative charges into atoms with positive charges.
6. Hydrogen atoms don't have neutrons.
7. Possible answers: hydrogen, oxygen, iron, silicon, helium, or carbon

Page 25

1. d
2. negative; positive
3. friction

4. Electricity

5. electrons; protons

6. attract; repel

7. Possible answer: Wool is a material that gains electrons easily. As the clothes tumbled in the dryer, friction caused the wool to gain lots of electrons. The atoms in the wool were attracted to the atoms in the pants, so the sock stuck to the pants.

Unifying Concepts and Processes

Possible answer: The atoms in the pieces of hair have lost electrons, so they all have positive charges. Atoms with the same charge repel each other, so the hairs repel each other and stick out in all directions.

Page 27

1. b

2. a

3. a

4. d

5. Possible answers: microwaves, radio waves

Page 29

1. b

2. d

3. Possible answer: a rock balanced at the top of a cliff

4. Possible answer: When the chemical bonds of food are changed by digestion, the energy stored in the food can be released.

5. potential; kinetic

6. You are storing energy in the spring and causing it to have potential energy.

Page 31

1. c

2. a

3. 2; 8; 18

4. Na, sodium; atomic number 11

5. Possible answer: An oxygen atom has six electrons in its outer shell. Each hydrogen atom has one electron. When these electrons are shared, the outer shell is filled with eight electrons.

Page 33

1. c

2. c

3. d

4. shiny; good conductors; react with oxygen

5. 80

6. Possible answer: Mercury is harder to find now because most of it has been mined from Earth's crust. Mercury is poisonous, so it's used more carefully than it once was.

7. Possible answer: The atoms and molecules in a solid are packed tightly together. They don't move out of the way when something touches them.

Page 35

1. d
2. Because molecules are packed together more tightly in water than they are in air.
3. The amplitude would decrease.
4. Answers will vary.
5. crest
6. trough
7. wavelength
8. amplitude

Page 36

1. A proton, neutron, and electron should be correctly labeled on the diagram.
2. b
3. d
4. a
5. c

Page 37

6. false
7. true
8. true
9. true
10. false
11. false
12. Electrons moving from one atom to another.
13. Protons have a positive charge, and electrons have a negative charge. The opposite charges pull toward one another.
14. It creates an electrical current.
15. Potential energy is energy that is stored and waiting to be used. Kinetic energy is the energy of an object in motion.
16. how many protons it has
17. It is liquid at room temperature.
18. metals; solids
19. a form of energy created by vibrations

Page 39

1. b
2. Many animals eat them. Some animals seek shelter in the mounds termites build or live in the mounds after the termites have abandoned them.

3. Possible answer: The birds perch on the rhinoceroses' backs and eat the parasites there. The birds get fed, and the rhinos get rid of their parasites.

4. Possible answer: A savanna is a tropical grassland. It has grasses, shrubs, and scattered trees. Animals such as lions, rhinoceroses, cheetahs, zebras, wildebeest, and ostriches live there.

5. They all work together and depend on one another. They allow the biome to function as a whole.

Page 41

1. d

2. d

3. The wolves attacked and killed livestock.

4. Possible answer: The population of elk grew larger because the wolves weren't hunting them. There wasn't enough for them to eat, so many starved. Coyotes became more widespread, and the animals they eat were hunted more heavily.

5. They live in a family pack, to which they are very loyal.

6. Answers will vary.

Page 43

1. b

2. Possible answer: Cacti are thick and don't have leaves. This means they have less surface area, so they don't lose much water into the air.

3. Possible answer: Trees have leaves. Each leaf adds to a plant's total surface area, so trees lose too much moisture to the air to survive in a dry desert.

4. Possible answer: They provide water, food, and habitat for several different kinds of animals.

5. Possible answer: The thorns protect the plants so animals can't easily eat them. Without this protection, the plant's life might be in danger.

Unifying Concepts and Processes

Possible answer: In the fall, many trees lose their leaves and become dormant for the winter. Less water is available because it is often frozen, and there isn't as much light because the days are shorter.

Page 45

1. pollen

2. stigma

3. depend

4. adapt

5. Possible answer: A hummingbird has a long, skinny beak that fits in the tube-like flower of the fuschia. There is no place to land on the fuschia, but hummingbirds don't need a landing pad.

6. pollinators

7. so that they can reproduce

8. Both the yucca plant and the moth benefit from the relationship. They need each other to survive.

9. the yucca moth

10. Possible answer: Yes, they coevolved. The yucca plant needs the moth in order to reproduce, and the moth's young feed on the plant's seeds.

Answer Key

Page 47

1. b
2. its size and its texture
3. Possible answer: An animal, like a bat, produces high-pitched sounds. The sounds bounce off objects around it. The bat uses this information to identify how large something is, where it is, what its texture is like, and whether it is moving.
4. A muscle in the ear keeps the sounds from being transmitted into the inner ear.
5. to help them move around in dark places, such as caves
6. moth

Unifying Concepts and Processes

Possible answer: Not all animals need echolocation because they don't hunt at night or live in dark environments. Other animals may have very good sight or sense of smell, or they may be fast runners.

Page 49

1. b
2. false
3. true
4. false
5. true
6. Possible answers: music, tripping over a rock, touching a piece of sandpaper
7. A pathway is created between neurons.
8. Possible answers: A voluntary action, like scratching your head, is something that is done by choice. An involuntary action, like blood flowing through your veins, is not under your control.
9. Possible answer: An impulse is an electrical signal that neurons send out when they are stimulated. This causes chemical neurotransmitters to be released.

Page 51

1. Possible answer: Both sets of twins are the result of a single pregnancy, so the babies have the same birthday. Identical twins look the same, while fraternal twins are no more similar than any other siblings.
2. Heredity is the passing along of genes and traits from one generation to the next.
3. because they have different life experiences as they grow older
4. Identical twins are identical because they come from the same fertilized egg. Fraternal twins come from two separate fertilized eggs.
5. false
6. true
7. false
8. false
9. true
10. false

Unifying Concepts and Processes

Possible answer: Scientists study identical twins that were separated because they have the same genes but different environments and experiences. There are others ways to study nature vs. nurture, but it would be hard to set up a better experiment. This way, scientists can tell how much of a role heredity plays in people's lives.

Page 52

1. c
2. d
3. a
4. b
5. b

Page 53

6. Scavengers eat the leftovers of the animals that predators kill.
7. Both a biome and a machine have many necessary parts that all work together.
8. Ranchers thought that the wolves would kill their livestock.
9. so they can tap into water deep underground
10. They don't have much surface area because they are thick and don't have leaves.
11. Possible answer: Bees eat the pollen and nectar from flowers. Some of the pollen sticks to their bodies. When they fly to the next flower, the pollen falls off and sticks to the flower's stigma.
12. Possible answer: An animal, like a bat, produces high-pitched sounds. The sounds bounce off objects around it. The bat uses this information to identify how large something is, where it is, what its texture is like, and whether it is moving.
13. They are the nerve cells of the body that send messages when they are stimulated.
14. draw a line to d
15. draw a line to c
16. draw a line to a
17. draw a line to f
18. draw a line to e
19. draw a line to b

Page 54

1. d
2. b
3. dominant
4. mechanical and chemical
5. Rocks need to be broken down into smaller pieces before they can be moved by water or wind.
6. Possible answer: The Wright Brothers built on the knowledge and work of other scientists and inventors when they invented their flying machine.
7. Possible answers: You should check with an adult to see if it is safe for you to do alone, and you should read the instructions.
8. protons and electrons
9. electromagnetic

Page 55

10. 13; 13

11. Possible answers: Wolves became endangered because human beings killed so many of them. They were reintroduced because they are a natural part of the Yellowstone ecosystem and many people felt they should be returned to their habitat.

12. Possible answer: All the animals in the savanna have a role to play. Losing even one species would have an effect on the other living creatures of the savanna.

13. The atoms in a solid are packed tightly together. In a liquid, they move more freely.

14. Flowers provide bees with food, and bees pollinate flowers so they can reproduce.

15. wind

16. to hunt or to make their way around in dark places

17. Scientists use (<u>data</u>, conclusions) to prove or disprove their ideas.

18. The (<u>Kelvin</u>, Celsius) temperature scale starts at absolute zero.

19. The Wright Brothers added a (propeller, <u>rudder</u>) to the tail of their flying machine.

20. Electricity is the movement of (protons, <u>electrons</u>) from one atom to another.

21. An ion is an atom with an electrical (<u>charge</u>, matter).

22. The highest point of a wave is the (trough, <u>crest</u>).

23. A child jumping rope is an example of (<u>kinetic</u>, potential) energy.

24. (<u>Fraternal</u>, Identical) twins are no more alike than any other pair of siblings.

25. The (central, <u>autonomic</u>) nervous system controls involuntary activities.

Page 57

1. c

2. c

3. b

4. Possible answer: The Cambrian Explosion was when the few life forms that existed on Earth suddenly evolved into many different kinds of organisms.

5. Possible answer: They need to use common names for the different time periods so there isn't confusion when they're discussing Earth's history.

Unifying Concepts and Processes

Possible answer: The edges of some continents look like they could fit together like pieces of a puzzle.

Page 59

1. c

2. b

3. d

4. Possible answer: The pieces in Earth's crust float on top of a layer of molten rock and slowly drift around the planet.

5. Possible answer: Earth's crust is the part that comes into contact with oxygen in the atmosphere.

Page 61

1. c

2. photosynthesis

3. Greenhouse gases

4. cycle

5. atmosphere

6. Possible answer: Greenhouse gases are good because they hold in the heat of the sun and make Earth warm enough to support life. Too many greenhouse gases aren't good for the environment because they make Earth warmer than it should be.

7. No, because human beings and animals need the oxygen that plants produce.

8. They use oxygen to help them release the energy stored in their food.

Unifying Concepts and Processes

Possible answer: The water cycle is similar to the oxygen cycle because the same series of events repeat themselves.

Page 63

1. c

2. d

3. a

4. toward the ocean

5. Possible answer: Air currents move from high-pressure areas to low-pressure areas, so storms aren't carried into areas of high pressure.

6. Possible answer: The warmer air at the equator rises into the upper atmosphere. The cooler air from the poles moves toward the equator to fill the space.

Page 65

1. a

2. b

3. According to the Ptolemaic system, Earth is at the center of the universe and the sun and planets move around it. In the heliocentric system, the sun is the center of our solar system.

4. The planets revolve, rotate, and tilt.

5. It changed the way people thought about the universe.

6. Possible answer: His ideas went against accepted religious teachings. Telescopes hadn't been invented yet, so it was hard to prove he was correct.

Unifying Concepts and Processes

Possible answer: Ptolemy's ideas were still important because they gave Copernicus and other scientists a starting place for their own theories. If Copernicus didn't believe Ptolemy was correct, he had to think about why and how to prove that something else was true instead.

Page 67

1. b

2. a

3. The asteroids are spread out over a huge area, so there's a lot of space between them.

4. Jupiter's strong gravity

5. Each comet has its own unique orbit around the sun.

6. Because another larger object was found beyond the Kuiper Belt.

Page 69

1. c

2. d

3. c

4. Possible answer: Unless you have an extremely powerful telescope, a galaxy and a star look almost the same.

5. Nebulae were actually galaxies containing millions of individual stars, and they were much farther away than anyone had ever thought possible.

6. Possible answer: *Nebula* used to refer to any light in the sky that didn't look like a regular star. Today, it is specifically a cloud of gas and dust where stars are born.

Page 70

1. a

2. c

3. c

4. d

5. Life on Earth became more complex and diverse.

6. oxygen

7. Because they float on a layer of molten rock.

Page 71

8. Plants use carbon dioxide and release oxygen during photosynthesis. Oxygen is used by human beings and animals, who then release carbon dioxide.

9. Greenhouse gases hold in Earth's heat. Too many greenhouse gases in the atmosphere increase the temperatures on Earth.

10. Copernicus believed Earth and the other planets orbit the sun.

11. Jupiter's gravity kept the asteroids from combining to form a planet.

12. A larger planet was discovered beyond Pluto. Instead of adding a tenth planet, scientists decided to call Pluto and the new discovery *dwarf planets*.

13. He saw that nebulae were actually collections of stars, and they were too far away to be part of our galaxy.

14. spiral

15. false

16. false

17. true

18. true

19. true

20. false

21. true

22. true

Page 73

1. d

2. a

3. pendulum

4. accurate

5. patterns

6. seismograph

7. Because the string absorbs the movement of the shaking ground

8. Possible answer: They can learn more about where earthquakes are likely to occur. They can build safer roads and buildings in these areas.

9. Possible answer: Several different seismographic stations send their results to one research station. The results are combined so that the exact location can be pinpointed.

Page 75

1. c

2. Possible answer: a long shelf life, extra flavor, resistant to insect pests

3. Possible answer: In selective breeding and GM crops, people are trying to change plants' characteristics. Selective breeding is a more natural way to do it. In GM crops, scientists can blend characteristics from different species—something that can't happen in nature.

4. Possible answer: They exist in nature. The wind, insects, and animals can carry pollen to other crops and fields.

5. Answers will vary.

Unifying Concepts and Processes

Possible answer: Large numbers of the insect would probably be killed. The animals that eat that insect might have to change their diet. If they ate another type of insect instead, its numbers might start to drop. Also, superinsects that weren't affected by the pest control might develop. They could be even harder to control.

Page 77

1. d

2. b

3. Possible answer: The light in a laser beam contains one wavelength and moves in one direction. The light from a light bulb contains many different wavelengths and spreads out in all directions.

4. Possible answer: Lasers can make very precise cuts. They are clean because only light touches the patient's body.

5. Possible answer: No, because a very specific mechanical device is used to make them.

Page 79

1. b

2. c

3. b

4. Possible answer: In six pages of text, some of the same letters would be used hundreds of times, so Gutenberg needed many copies of each letter.

Unifying Concepts and Processes

Possible answer: Part of the scientific method is to share the results of research. Gutenberg's press made that easier, so scientific knowledge spread much more quickly around the world. When scientific research is put on the Internet, it can be seen instantly by scientists everywhere.

Page 81

1. true

2. false

3. false

4. true

5. an Earth-observing satellite

6. a moon

7. The operators will shut it off. It will eventually start to fall back toward Earth and burn up in the atmosphere.

8. Possible answers: Both orbit Earth. Only human-made satellites gather information and send it back to Earth.

9. A GPS receives signals from a navigation satellite that shows its exact location.

10. The launch of the Soviet satellite *Sputnik* kicked off the beginning of the space race.

11. Possible answer: Satellites can be useful for the military because they can't be seen from Earth with the naked eye, which makes them especially good for performing spy work.

Page 83

1. b

2. Possible answer: Early photographers needed a lot of equipment and used dangerous chemicals. People using Eastman's cameras just took the pictures and the company did the rest.

3. Possible answer: Celluloid film was less expensive. Celluloid was lighter than copper or glass and lasted longer than paper.

4. Possible answer: Too much or too little light would ruin the picture.

5. Possible answer: Traditional cameras use film, but digital cameras use electric panels.

6. Possible answer: Both traditional and digital cameras use light to produce photographs.

Page 85

1. It allowed people to travel from place to place without getting stuck in mud or ruts.

2. traffic; weather

3. Possible answer: Asphalt is cheaper and easier to repair, but concrete is stronger and lasts longer.

4. Possible answer: If they don't have good drainage systems, they can buckle or collapse when the ground becomes filled with water.

5. Possible answer: A good system of roads meant that information and goods could spread quickly through the empire.

6. They can keep the concrete from cracking and hold it together if it does.

7. Possible answer: Yes, roads probably had to be much stronger to stand the weight of cars. Roads would have had increased traffic. People would also have been able to travel farther, so new roads would have been needed to be built.

Page 86

1. b
2. c
3. d
4. Use more than one seismograph.
5. Possible answers: A GM crop can resist damage done by insects or disease. If a certain insect has nothing to eat and dies out, all the animals above it in the food chain might be affected as well.
6. Lasers are clean and precise cutting tools.
7. A laser that cuts metal is very hot, but a laser that is used in eye surgery is not.

Page 87

8. Gutenberg's press used pieces of type that could be moved around.
9. After the printing press was invented, information could be shared more quickly.
10. Weather satellites are used to track storms and clouds. Communication satellites send and receive messages from Earth.
11. Yes, the bolt is a piece of space debris.
12. Daguerreotypes used expensive copper plates, and the images were easy to damage.
13. If the ground below a road gets too wet, it becomes soft and the road can collapse.
14. Sturdy roads needed to be built because wheels form ruts in dirt and mud.
15. seismic waves
16. type
17. wavelength
18. celluloid
19. atmosphere
20. asphalt

Page 89

1. d
2. d
3. They were a place for people to clean themselves and to socialize.
4. They rubbed the dirt off with a dry towel.
5. Possible answer: Personal hygiene helps people stay healthy and feel good about themselves. It can also stop the spread of illness.
6. Possible answer: He noticed that medical students had contact with both sick people and the women who were going to give birth. He realized that the students were carrying the infections to the women.
7. Hand-washing stops germs from spreading.

Page 91

1. b
2. d
3. IL
4. FL
5. FL
6. IL
7. It could allow a virus to enter your computer.
8. You don't have any way of knowing whether people are who they say they are online.
9. They can help protect you when you are online.

Page 93

1. c
2. d
3. c
4. Possible answer: Water stored in a reservoir can be used as a recreational area.
5. Possible answer: Solar power wouldn't work very well on a cloudy day.
6. Answers will vary.

Page 95

1. b
2. true
3. false
4. true
5. false
6. Possible answer: Human beings eat the large predator fish that consume plants and smaller fish in the ocean.
7. Possible answers: They are high in protein, low in fat, and contain healthy omega-3 fatty acids.
8. Bioaccumulation is the buildup of chemicals in the body over time.
9. Large fish eat more than smaller fish do. They also end up consuming all the toxins that the smaller fish eat.

Page 97

1. b
2. a
3. Air that has been heated during the summer rises and pulls the moist air inland.
4. Possible answer: They have chopped down trees, which causes erosion to take place more quickly.

Unifying Concepts and Processes

Possible answer: The land in a delta is flat, so Hurricane Katrina's winds sent tall, strong waves across the land. They flooded the area and caused a lot of damage.

Page 99

1. c
2. a
3. human beings' use of fossil fuels
4. Because carbon dioxide is a greenhouse gas, and too many greenhouse gases in the atmosphere contribute to global warming.
5. The ocean was getting closer to the lighthouse and would have destroyed it.

Unifying Concepts and Processes

Possible answer: No change in nature affects only one organism. The lives of plants and animals are connected to one another. Another example of this is found in the selection about reintroducing wolves to Yellowstone. Many species of animals were affected when the wolves disappeared and when they returned.

Page 101

1. c
2. true
3. false
4. true
5. true
6. false
7. They made many people consider whether the risk of space travel to human beings was worth it.
8. Possible answer: Using robots is safer and less expensive, but robots can't do everything human beings can do.
9. Possible answer: They believe that there are many problems on Earth and that the money should be spent to help solve those problems.
10. Answers will vary.

Page 102

1. c
2. d
3. true
4. false
5. true
6. false
7. true
8. true
9. false
10. Possible answer: Personal hygiene is keeping your body clean and healthy. It helps you feel good about yourself and keeps germs from spreading.

Page 103

11. Greeks and Romans bathed in public, but we bathe in private today.

12. Possible answer: Only after you have asked an adult to be sure it is safe

13. Possible answer: Wind is a clean source of energy, and it will always be available.

14. Because solar cells are expensive to make compared to the energy they produce.

15. Because they eat lots of smaller fish that have been contaminated.

16. Fish is a low-fat, high-protein food. Eating too much of certain kinds of fish can pose a risk to your health because they contain toxins.

17. Possible answers: It rains a lot, and because the land is already wet in Bangladesh, there is a lot of flooding and illness.

18. Bangladesh is flat, so the waves coming onshore flood the land. The high winds damage buildings.

19. We burn too many fossil fuels.

20. Possible answer: Scientists may be able to find alternative fuel sources in outer space. One day, human beings might be able to live on the moon or another planet.

21. the explosions of the *Challenger* and *Columbia* space shuttles

Page 105

1. a
2. b
3. 3
4. 1
5. 5
6. 2
7. 4
8. The movement of water molecules pushed the pollen around.
9. Possible answer: Both Einstein and Dalton worked with atoms and built on the work of other scientists.

Unifying Concepts and Processes

Possible answer: Atoms are extremely tiny and can't be seen even with a microscope, so proving they existed was a very difficult process.

Page 107

1. a
2. c
3. Alhazen wrote that vision was caused by rays entering the eyes, not by rays the eyes sent out.
4. Possible answer: Thousands of people brought new ideas about science and art with them when they traveled to the big cities for trade or religion.
5. Possible answer: The scholars of the Islamic Empire used ideas they learned from the Greeks and Romans. Then, scientists during the Renaissance used knowledge they learned from the Islamic scientists.
6. Possible answer: New medical discoveries weren't made very often, so a book containing as much information as Avicenna's had in it was useful for a long time.

Page 109

1. b

2. Possible answer: Machines can work much longer without a break than human beings can.

3. Possible answer: Machines could be used anywhere because steam engines didn't need to be located by running water.

4. Possible answer: More work could be done with less effort, so prices for many goods fell. Machines and engines produced pollution.

5. Possible answer: Something needed to be burned to create the heat that boiled water and produced steam. Whatever was being burned—wood or coal—produced the pollution.

6. When steam power was used in the printing industry, reading material became more affordable and available, and more people learned to read.

Page 111

1. a

2. c

3. Water was used to transport people and goods around the world, so it was more convenient to be near the water.

4. Possible answer: Cars don't need to eat or sleep, so they can travel much farther without stopping.

5. Possible answer: The shuttle does not have to move over or through air or ground, so there is nothing to slow it down.

Page 113

1. b

2. d

3. They found that people didn't want to buy what they were growing.

4. He came up with dozens of ways to use peanuts and sweet potatoes.

5. Possible answer: Most scientists carefully record their results and share the information they've found with other scientists.

6. Possible answer: Progress would be very slow because scientists would not be able to build upon the work of others.

7. Boll weevils

8. alternative

9. agriculture

Page 115

1. false

2. true

3. true

4. false

5. true

6. Carson was a strong writer, and this helped her share her message with the public.

7. Possible answer: Carson was criticizing their products. They were worried they would lose money.

8. It was the beginning of the environmental movement.

Answer Key

9. Answers will vary.

Unifying Concepts and Processes

1. Possible answer: They would both be concerned about the effect of pesticides on human beings and on the food chain.

2. Possible answer: Yes. If the chemicals don't break down easily, animals higher up on the food chain could have higher concentrations of toxins inside them.

Page 117

1. b

2. d

3. Possible answer: The graphics used to be very simple, but now they look more realistic.

4. Possible answer: As computer hardware and software got better, they were used in video games, too.

5. Possible answer: Hardware got smaller, and software got more powerful.

6. Possible answer: Since people were willing to pay for video game systems, companies thought it was worth the money to invent better ones.

Page 118

1. b

2. c

3. d

4. c

5. electrons

6. scientific method

7. Possible answer: the *camera obscura*

Page 119

8. Possible answer: Steam engines could be used anywhere. This meant that machines didn't need to be near moving water in order to operate, so factories could be built anywhere.

9. Possible answer: Steam engines allowed people to travel more quickly, and goods became less expensive to produce and purchase.

10. Water moving in a river could carry people quickly from place to place.

11. He advised them to rotate their crops.

12. peanuts, sweet potatoes

13. He didn't write them down or share them with other scientists.

14. She was afraid DDT would kill all the songbirds.

15. Possible answer: It started the environmental movement and made people aware of the dangers of pesticide use.

16. Possible answer: hardware and software

17. draw a line to d

18. draw a line to f

19. draw a line to a

20. draw a line to g

21. draw a line to e

22. draw a line to b

23. draw a line to c

Page 120

1. a

2. d

3. b

4. d

5. b

Page 121

6. Scientists gather (<u>data</u>, conclusions) to prove or disprove hypotheses.

7. Two (dominant, <u>recessive</u>) genes will produce the trait of the recessive gene.

8. Positive charges (<u>repel</u>, attract) other positive charges.

9. A person skiing down a mountain is an example of (potential, <u>kinetic</u>) energy.

10. Sound moves faster through (<u>solids</u>, gases) than through liquids.

11. *Echolocation* is the use of (hertz, <u>vibrations</u>) to locate objects.

12. The (<u>autonomic</u>, peripheral) nervous system controls involuntary activities.

13. Wind is caused by differences in (chemicals, <u>temperature</u>) in Earth's atmosphere.

14. Erosion is the movement of soil and rock by wind, water, or ice.

15. Possible answers: Fahrenheit, Celsius, Kelvin

16. Possible answer: Many people contributed to both discoveries.

17. Possible answer: Don't eat or drink in the lab, and wear safety glasses when necessary.

18. Possible answers: light, radio waves, microwaves

19. Elements can't be broken down because they contain only one kind of atom

20. They depend on one another—they are interdependent.

21. Farmers hunted them because they were killing livestock. They've been reintroduced because they are part of the ecosystem and help keep it balanced.

Page 122

22. The species adapt to one another over time.

23. neurons

24. Nature refers to genes and heredity, and nurture refers to the effects of the environment.

25. Earth's crust is divided into plates, and it is thinner under the oceans than on land.

26. the burning of fossil fuels

27. Plants use carbon dioxide in Earth's atmosphere to make food, and then they produce oxygen as a waste product.

28. Possible answers: asteroids, centaurs, comets, dwarf planets

29. shape

30. Milky Way

31. earthquakes

32. Possible answer: The printing press helped information spread through Europe. Scientists during the Renaissance used knowledge that was discovered by Islamic scientists.

33. Possible answer: Don't download programs or files from sources you don't trust.

34. Traditional cameras use chemical film. Digital cameras use electrical devices.

35. wear from weather and traffic

Page 123

36. Possible answer: Solar power doesn't create air pollution, but solar cells won't work on a cloudy day.

37. Fish higher on the food chain eat many smaller fish that have been contaminated.

38. 4, 2, 5, 1, 3

39. true

40. true

41. false

42. true

43. false

44. true

45. true

46. draw a line to b

47. draw a line to e

48. draw a line to d

49. draw a line to a

50. draw a line to f

51. draw a line to c